To my mother, Mrs. Sushila Kujur,
who, at 70, remains a force of unwavering strength—energetic,
disciplined, and ever watchful.
Like the strictest of teachers, she has shaped me with her firm
hand and steadfast spirit.
This book is a tribute to her enduring guidance, her commanding
presence, and the silent love that has anchored my journey—
from body to soul.

BODY AND SOUL: THE ETERNAL COMPANIONS

REDISCOVERING THE LOVE THAT HAS ALWAYS BEEN WITH YOU

TITUS NAZARENE KUJUR

Contents

Contents

Preface

Body and Soul: The Eternal Companions

There is a quiet truth that lives beneath all the noise of the world:

You are never truly alone.

Not in the stillness of early morning, nor in the aching silence of loss. Not in your laughter, your longing, or your fear. Even when no other hand reaches for yours, even when no voice calls your name, something within you has always been there—breathing, witnessing, waiting.

This book is an offering to that presence.

To the one who wakes with you and aches with you.

To the one who carries you across years and dreams, pain and joy.

To the body that holds your life.

To the soul that holds your truth.

Together, they are your oldest companions.

We live in a time where we are often taught to treat the body as a machine and the soul as a mystery we might never understand. But what if neither is a problem to be solved, a puzzle to unlock, or a vessel to be perfected? What if both are sacred partners—guiding you, speaking to you, and yearning to be known not through judgment, but through friendship?

Body and Soul: The Eternal Companions is not a manual. It is a remembering. A soft return to what has always been within you. Through its pages, you will not be given rigid instructions or quick fixes. Instead, you will be invited into conversation—with your breath, your feelings, your weariness, your wonder. You will be asked to listen deeply. To rest. To tell the truth. To ask your body how it feels and your soul what it needs.

You will be asked to believe that both matter.

Each chapter holds space for something many of us were never taught: how to live with ourselves in wholeness. Not as fragmented identities torn between duty and desire, but as beings worthy of tending—worthy of stillness, joy, boundaries, grief, and belonging.

If you've ever felt numb, restless, unseen, or disconnected from yourself, this book is not here to fix you. It is here to remind you: nothing within you is broken. Your body still speaks, even when you don't listen. Your soul still dreams, even when you've forgotten how. And beneath every doubt, your essence waits with quiet patience for your return.

This is a journey of sacred reconnection.
This is a letter to your most loyal companions.
This is your invitation to come home.

May these pages offer you warmth in your solitude, courage in your questions, and light in the places you thought were dark. May they help you remember: the breath is your prayer, the body is your altar, and the soul—oh, the soul—is your eternal witness.

Welcome home.

With tenderness,
Titus Nazarene Kujur

Prologue

Body and Soul: The Eternal Companions

We often search for companionship in the external world—yearning for someone who will stay, listen, understand, and walk beside us through the changing seasons of life. Yet we overlook the oldest companions we've ever known: the body that has carried us since birth, and the soul that has waited quietly within, offering its silent wisdom.

This book is not a roadmap to escape yourself. It is a gentle invitation to return home.

For many of us, our relationship with our body has been complicated—judged, ignored, or overworked. Our soul, too, has often been forgotten in the noise of survival, buried beneath expectations and distractions. But neither has ever abandoned you. Not in your joy. Not in your loneliness. Not even in your silence. They remain your truest allies—ever faithful, ever near.

This book is about learning to befriend your own aliveness. To treat your body not as a burden to fix, but as a temple of wisdom and sensation. To listen to your soul not as a mystery to decode, but as the whisper of the infinite within. When we learn to honor both, we begin to heal from the inside out.

The journey you are about to take is not linear. It is not a climb. It is a soft unfolding—like petals opening to light, like breath remembering how to slow down. Each chapter is a door into deeper awareness, offering you reflections, practices, and truths to help you live in greater harmony with yourself.

Because you were never truly alone.

Your body remembers. Your soul waits.

And now, together, they call you back—to listen, to feel, to know, and to love the one companion who has always been with you: your Self.

ONE

THE COMPANIONS YOU NEVER NOTICED

You are never truly alone—not in your joy, not in your grief, not even in silence. The body breathes with you, the soul waits within you. Always.

There comes a moment in every life when the crowd disappears, the phone stops ringing, and the applause fades into memory. In that silence, you are left with one undeniable presence: yourself. And yet, how many of us truly know what that means?

When you strip away the layers of external identity—your job, your family roles, your social labels, your digital persona—what remains? It's not a void. It is not emptiness. It is a space occupied by your two oldest, most loyal companions: your **body** and your **soul**. They are not simply parts of you; they *are* you. They have been with you since the first breath and will remain until the last—and perhaps, even beyond.

Yet we treat them like strangers. We push our body to exhaustion, curse it when it doesn't look the way we want, neglect it when we are too busy, punish it with toxic habits. We ignore the soul altogether, dismissing its whispers as irrational feelings, sentimental nonsense, or inconvenient truths. In chasing acceptance, we abandon ourselves. In seeking love, we ignore the ones who love us most.

This book begins with an invitation to reconnect—to recognize that **your body and soul are not burdens to manage but companions to cherish**. It is not new knowledge; it's ancient wisdom we have forgotten. The sages knew it. The poets knew it. Children know it—until we teach them otherwise.

Reclaiming the Forgotten Friendship

Think back to your childhood. When you were hurt, you cried without shame. When you were tired, you slept without guilt. When you were hungry, you ate with delight. You trusted your body. You listened to your inner voice. You danced, sang, rested, played—all without needing a reason or permission. You were not at war with yourself. You were at peace.

Somewhere along the way, conditioning crept in. You learned that crying was weakness, rest was laziness, hunger was to be controlled, feelings were irrational, and joy had to be earned. You were taught to distrust your own body and silence your own soul. That disconnection has consequences. Anxiety, depression, burnout, chronic illness—these are not random afflictions. They are signals from within, signs that something essential has been forgotten.

But there is hope. You can return. You can begin again. You can rebuild the relationship with your body and soul—not through perfection or discipline, but through kindness, attention, and truth.

The Body: Your Earthly Home

Your body is not a project to be perfected. It is your **home**. Every breath you take is a reminder that it chooses life for you again and again. Your heartbeat is a rhythm that plays in the background, tirelessly, asking nothing in return. When you fall, it heals you. When you tire, it asks you to rest. It is always communicating with you—through fatigue, pain, hunger, goosebumps, tears. But have you been listening?

To love your body is not vanity. It is gratitude. To rest when tired is not laziness. It is wisdom. Your body has weathered storms you don't even remember. It has carried the weight of your stress, your secrets, your heartbreaks. It has shown up for you every single day. Can you show up for it?

This friendship begins with acknowledgment. Stand before a mirror, not to judge but to witness. Look at the lines, the scars, the textures, the curves. Each one tells a story. Each one is proof that you have lived. Offer your body your attention, your patience, your kindness. It will respond. It always has.

The Soul: The Silent Witness

If your body is your home, then your soul is the **light inside**. It is not something you have to earn or develop. It is not something outside you. Your soul is the quiet observer within—the one who watches your thoughts, your fears, your dreams. It is the part of you that knows right from wrong, not because of a rule book, but because of a feeling.

Have you ever sat in silence and felt a strange peace you couldn't explain? Or met someone who made you feel seen without a word? Or visited a place that felt like home even though you'd never been there before? That is your soul recognizing truth.

While the world changes around you, your soul remains unchanged. It is not bound by titles or appearances. It is not impressed by success or fame. It seeks authenticity. It thrives on presence. And it waits for you—always. You don't need to be spiritual or religious to connect with your soul. You only need to be *honest.*

When you lie to yourself, your soul feels heavy. When you betray your values, it aches. When you honour your truth, it sings. Learn to notice these cues. Learn to trust them. Your soul is your compass, not your critic.

Loneliness Is a Lie

You may have felt alone at times—perhaps abandoned, unseen, or misunderstood. That pain is real. But the idea that you were ever *truly* alone is not. Even in your darkest hour, your breath stayed. Your pulse continued. Your soul whispered, even if you couldn't hear it. The reason you're still here is because **they** never gave up on you.

The world may forget you. Friends may leave. Lovers may betray. But your body and soul will not. They do not need you to be rich, successful, attractive, or clever. They only ask that you be **present**.

So, the next time you feel alone, do not reach outward. Reach inward. Place your hand on your heart. Feel its rhythm. That is the sound of a loyal friend who never left.

Daily Practices to Reconnect

Rebuilding this friendship requires intention, not perfection. Start small:

- **Morning Check-In**: Before you reach for your phone, place your hand on your belly. Take three deep breaths. Ask yourself: How do I feel?
- **Mirror Practice**: Look at yourself in the mirror. Say something kind. It can be simple: *"Thank you for showing up today."*
- **Body Scan**: Sit quietly. Close your eyes. Move your attention from the top of your head to your toes. Notice any tension or sensation. Don't judge—just notice.
- **Soul Journal**: Write one honest sentence a day. Not what you *should* feel—what you *do* feel. Even if it's "I don't know what I feel."
- **Stillness Practice**: Sit in silence for 5 minutes. Breathe. Don't try to clear your mind. Just be.

These simple acts are signals. They tell your body and soul: *I see you. I hear you. I am with you.* That is the beginning of love.

What This Book Will Offer

This chapter is just the beginning. In the chapters ahead, we will explore:

- How to speak your body's language
- How to hear the voice of your soul
- How to navigate heartbreak, grief, and betrayal without abandoning yourself

- How to deal with fear, shame, guilt, and self-doubt
- How to reclaim joy, confidence, and inner peace
- How to live from a place of wholeness

Each chapter is a step in this inner journey—a return to yourself.

You don't need to be fixed. You need to be met. You don't need to find your worth. You need to remember it. You don't need a guru. You already have one within.

Let this be the first day of a new relationship—the one between you and the companions you never noticed.

Your body. Your soul. Your oldest friends.

And from this point forward, you will never walk alone again.

TWO

THE VOICE OF THE BODY

"Your body whispers before it screams. Listen early."

If the soul is the silent witness within, then the body is the ever-speaking messenger. It never ceases to communicate. From the flutter of anxiety in your stomach before a difficult conversation to the exhaustion that hits you after too many nights without rest, your body speaks in its own quiet, persistent language. But have you learned to listen?

For many of us, the answer is no. We have been conditioned to override, suppress, and silence the voice of the body. We are told to "push through," "tough it out," "ignore the pain," "sleep when you're dead," and "no pain, no gain." These mantras, though rooted in a culture that prizes achievement and endurance, often come at a cost: disconnection, dysfunction, and disease.

The Language of Sensation

The body speaks in sensations. Not in words, but in feelings. Tension. Tingling. Warmth. Shivers. Tightness. A racing heart. Dry mouth. A sinking feeling in your gut. A rush of energy. A sudden stillness. These sensations are not random. They are information. Your body is constantly scanning your environment, your relationships, your thoughts, and your choices—and it reports back to you through these cues.

When you meet someone who feels unsafe, your chest may tighten. When you walk into a place that feels peaceful, your breath slows down. When you're about to make a choice that doesn't align with your truth, your stomach knots. This is not irrational. This is ancient intelligence. Your body has been shaped by millennia of evolution to protect, alert, and guide you.

The more you learn to notice these cues, the more you will understand what your body is trying to tell you. This is not about hyper-vigilance or paranoia. It's about presence. It's about learning to treat every ache, every flutter, every sigh as a messenger, not a nuisance.

Ignored Signals Become Symptoms

When you ignore your body's voice, it doesn't stop speaking—it just speaks louder. That tightness in your neck after a stressful day? If unacknowledged, it might become chronic tension. That persistent fatigue you brush off as normal? It may grow into burnout. That mild indigestion you dismiss? Over time, it might evolve into digestive issues.

The body is patient, but not passive. If whispers don't work, it will begin to speak in aches, inflammation, stiffness, and eventually, illness. Many chronic conditions begin as unattended whispers. But the good news is that the body is also remarkably forgiving. The moment you begin to listen, it begins to respond.

Pain is not punishment. It's a signal. Fatigue is not weakness. It's a need. Hunger is not a flaw. It's feedback. These are not problems to fix; they are messages to understand.

Learning the Body's Vocabulary

Start with the basics. Ask yourself:

- When do I feel most energized?
- What foods make me feel light, and what makes me sluggish?
- Where do I hold tension when I'm anxious?
- How does my body feel after spending time with certain people?
- What does tired feel like *before* I collapse?
- What does *no* feel like in my body? What does *yes* feel like?

You don't need to have scientific answers. You only need to start noticing patterns. Awareness always precedes transformation.

Begin to observe without judgment. If your shoulders rise when you're stressed, don't scold them. Just notice. If your stomach churns before meetings, acknowledge it. If your jaw clenches during conflict, name it. Your job is not to control the body, but to become fluent in its language.

The Instinctual Body

Beyond sensations, your body also holds instinct. That gut feeling that someone is lying. That shiver down your spine before danger. That unexplainable sense that you're on the wrong path. These are not delusions. They are primal truths.

Modern society has prized intellect over instinct, logic over intuition. We've come to believe that only what can be measured is valid. But the body knows in ways the mind cannot. Science is only now beginning to understand what our ancestors knew through experience—that the body has its own wisdom.

There are nerves in your gut that function like a second brain. Your heart has an electromagnetic field that can synchronize with others nearby. Trauma, joy, and memory are stored in your tissues, not just your mind. Your posture, breath, and facial expressions constantly affect your emotions and perceptions.

The body is not separate from the mind or soul. It is their vehicle, their interface, their expression. When you ignore it, you cut off access to a deep well of insight. When you honour it, you open a channel to your most authentic self.

Reconnecting with the Body

So how do you begin to listen? You start small. You start gently. Here are some daily practices to invite this connection:

1. **Body Check-In**: Several times a day, pause and ask: *What sensations am I feeling right now?* Label them without judgment.
2. **Movement as Inquiry**: Rather than exercise as punishment, explore movement as a way to feel. Try stretching, dancing, or walking—not to achieve a result, but to meet your body.

3. **Breath Awareness**: Your breath is the bridge between body and mind. Spend five minutes each day simply noticing your breath. Is it shallow? Deep? Fast? Uneven? Let it be whatever it is.
4. **Touch with Intention**: Place a hand on your chest or belly and breathe. Offer your body the comfort you would give a child.
5. **Eat with Presence**: Choose one meal a day to eat slowly, without distraction. Notice the texture, the flavour, how your body feels before, during, and after.
6. **Rest Without Guilt**: Schedule ten minutes to lie down, eyes closed, without doing anything. Let your body feel what it feels.

These are not rituals of luxury. They are practices of homecoming. Your body has waited patiently. Now, you begin to show up.

Emotional Signals in the Body

Every emotion you feel is mirrored in the body. Anxiety tightens the chest. Sadness sinks the shoulders. Joy lifts the face. Anger heats the limbs. When we repress emotions, they don't disappear—they lodge in the body. Chronic tension, stiffness, and even autoimmune conditions can stem from unreleased emotional energy.

To listen to the body is to listen to emotion. You don't need to analyse or solve it. Just feel it. Emotions are like weather—they pass more quickly when allowed to move.

Try this:

- The next time you feel anxious, ask: *Where is this in my body?*
- Place your attention there. Breathe into it. Say: *I feel you. I'm here.*
- Do not try to change the feeling. Simply allow it to exist.

This is emotional presence. It is one of the deepest forms of self-care.

Trusting the Body's Yes and No

Your body knows what it wants. It also knows what it doesn't. The more you listen, the clearer it becomes.

A *yes* might feel like openness, warmth, energy, ease. A *no* might feel like contraction, heaviness, resistance, or nausea. These signals are subtle, but consistent. Over time, they become unmistakable.

When facing a choice—whether to take a job, end a relationship, or speak your truth—ask your body. Sit in stillness. Imagine each option. Notice how your body responds. Your body's answer may not align with your logic, but it is always aligned with your truth.

This does not mean every hard thing is wrong. Growth often feels uncomfortable. But even then, there is a difference between fear that signals growth and fear that signals danger. The former feels electric; the latter feels suffocating.

You already know how to discern this. You've always known. Listening to your body is about remembering.

Rewriting the Narrative

You have inherited many beliefs about the body. That it must look a certain way. That its desires are dangerous. That its needs are inconvenient. That its aging is shameful. These are cultural stories, not truths.

You can write a new story. One where the body is a sacred partner, not a problem to fix. One where wrinkles are wisdom, curves are creativity, scars are survival, and needs are natural.

You do not owe the world thinness, youth, or perfection. You owe your body only love, honesty, and care. When you offer these, the body begins to heal. And as it heals, so do you.

When Listening Is Hard

Sometimes, listening to the body is painful—especially if you have experienced trauma. The body may feel unsafe. Sensations may trigger fear. Presence may bring up past pain.

This is not failure. It is part of the journey. Go slowly. Go gently. You do not have to force anything. You can work with a therapist, a somatic coach, or a healer. You can start with small moments of contact: a breath, a touch, a moment of stillness.

The goal is not to feel good all the time. The goal is to feel *truthfully*—and to let that truth guide you.

The Aligned Life

An aligned life begins with an aligned body. When you listen to your hunger, you nourish. When you rest when tired, you renew. When you express your emotions, you release. When you move with joy, you revive. When you trust your instincts, you return to your path.

This is not self-indulgence. This is self-respect. This is how you become whole.

You don't need to live perfectly. You need to live *in relationship*. With your body. With your soul. With your truth.

Final Thoughts for This Chapter

Your body is not an obstacle to be overcome. It is not a decoration to be displayed. It is a sacred, sentient, wise being that has only ever wanted your attention.

It has endured your absence. It has absorbed your pain. It has carried your dreams. It has waited for your return.

Today, begin again.

Place your hand on your heart. Take a deep breath. Whisper: *I'm listening now.*

And your body will whisper back: *Welcome home.*

THREE

The Whisper of the Soul

"And when you are silent enough, still enough, surrendered enough—there it is. The soul speaks not in thunder, but in whispers. You must learn how to hear it."

Introduction: Hearing Beyond the Noise

In a world drowning in noise—the noise of opinions, duties, deadlines, and distractions—the voice of the soul can seem like the faintest of echoes, often lost in the daily clamour. But it is always there, waiting for you. It speaks softly, calmly, and patiently. Unlike the body, which speaks through aches and pulses, the soul communicates through the subtle languages of intuition, stillness, dreams, and inner knowing.

To hear the whisper of the soul, one must choose silence—not necessarily the absence of sound, but the presence of awareness. This chapter is an invitation to remember who you are beneath the thoughts, roles, and ambitions. It is a guide to reconnecting with your essence, the quiet truth that never left.

The Nature of the Soul

The soul is not a concept to be understood intellectually—it is to be felt, encountered, remembered. Some call it the Higher Self, the Inner Light, or the Divine Spark. It is the quiet observer within you, the eternal witness who remains unshaken by change. Where the body is mortal and the mind restless, the soul is timeless, infinite, and wise.

When you are in tune with your soul, life no longer feels like a chaotic chase. It becomes a dance, one where every step has meaning, every turn has grace, and even stumbles lead you somewhere true. The soul does not scream for your attention. It waits for you to become still enough to listen.

Recognizing Soul-Language

How does one listen to something so subtle? How does one identify when the soul is speaking?

Let us explore the unique forms in which the soul communicates.

1. Intuition – The Gentle Nudge

Intuition is the soul's compass. It doesn't justify, argue, or analyse. It simply *knows*. It may come as a gut feeling, a sudden insight, or an inexplicable certainty. You may feel drawn to a path that seems illogical but feels deeply right. That is the whisper of your soul guiding you—not toward comfort, but toward growth and alignment.

Philosophers and mystics have long revered intuition as sacred knowledge. Descartes doubted everything except the mind. But even he could not doubt the intuitive clarity of the soul's awareness. Intuition is your soul's candle in the fog of mental chatter.

2. Deep Peace – The Soul's Signature

The soul resides in stillness. You'll recognize its presence not in adrenaline but in peace. When you make a decision aligned with your soul, even if it involves sacrifice, it brings with it a profound calm. This peace cannot be found in material gain, approval, or external success. It arises from authenticity—living in harmony with your inner truth.

When you say no to what drains you and yes to what nourishes your spirit, peace flows. When you stop performing and start being, the soul rejoices. This deep peace is your soul clapping softly.

3. Inner Knowing – The Voice Without Words

The soul does not always speak in language. Sometimes it speaks through a knowing that bypasses reason. You might not know *how* you know, but you do. This knowing is subtle but unwavering. Unlike beliefs that can be debated or shaken, inner knowing is rooted in your being.

For example, a child intuitively knows when a person is unsafe. A person standing before a great mountain *knows* they are in the presence of something greater than themselves. This is not taught. It is felt. It is soul memory.

4. Dreams – The Soul's Imagery

The soul often communicates through dreams—not just the nocturnal variety, but also our waking visions and longings. Dreams carry symbols, metaphors, and messages that the conscious mind might overlook. In your dreams, the soul weaves together truth, longing, and reflection.

That recurring dream of flying? It may be your soul reminding you of freedom. The forgotten face you keep seeing? Perhaps your soul nudging you toward unresolved emotions or latent desires. In dreams, the soul paints what words cannot express.

The Obstructions to Soul Listening

If the soul is always whispering, why do so few hear it?

The answer lies in the way we have been conditioned. From childhood, we are taught to trust authority, logic, and external validation. Feelings are dismissed as irrational. Stillness is labelled laziness. Instinct is overshadowed by social expectation. The result? We begin to live outside ourselves, relying on noise to tell us who we are.

There are common barriers to soul-hearing:

- **Mental clutter**: Overthinking drowns out the subtle inner voice.
- **Fear**: The soul often guides us to leap—something the ego resists.
- **Busyness**: Constant activity prevents introspection.
- **Disconnection from nature**: The soul thrives in still, organic spaces.

- **Addiction to control**: The soul calls for surrender, not dominance.

To reconnect with your soul, you must unlearn. You must declutter the mind and cleanse the heart. Soul-hearing is not about becoming more—it is about becoming less so that truth can enter.

Soul Practices: Hearing the Whisper

Let us now explore practices that help you hear the whisper of the soul.

1. Sacred Silence

Set aside time each day to be completely silent. No music, no phone, no talking. Just you and your breath. In this silence, observe. Don't *try* to hear the soul. Simply be present. Let thoughts come and go. With time, a different voice will emerge—quieter, kinder, wiser.

2. Contemplative Journaling

Ask your soul questions. Write down whatever arises without judgment. Some questions to begin with:

- "What am I ignoring in myself?"
- "What is something I need to release?"
- "What would I do if I weren't afraid?"

Often, the first answers are from the mind. But as you keep writing, you'll notice deeper insights emerge.

3. Dream Work

Keep a dream journal. Each morning, write down any dreams you recall. Look for patterns or recurring symbols. Ask yourself what feelings those images evoke. Over time, you'll begin to decode the soul's dream-language.

4. Spiritual Reading and Solitude

Spend time with poetry, sacred texts, or writings that stir your inner world. Not for knowledge—but for resonance. The soul recognizes truth through resonance. Also, retreat into solitude. Spend a day, a weekend, or even an hour alone in nature or a quiet space. Solitude invites the soul to speak.

The Soul in Decision Making

How can you bring soul-listening into your life decisions?
Here's a practice:
When faced with a choice, ask yourself:

- "Which option feels light, expansive, peaceful?"
- "Which choice makes me feel like I'm coming home to myself?"

Then sit with the silence. Let the answer come without force. The mind wants certainty; the soul offers clarity. Not always immediate, but always right.

Even when the soul-guided choice is harder on the surface, it will feel *right*. The deeper self is always drawn to truth, not comfort. The soul does not promise ease, but it guarantees meaning.

The Soul and Suffering

Often, the soul speaks most clearly through suffering. When we stray too far from our essence, pain arises—not as punishment, but as redirection. Heartbreak, loss, disillusionment—they strip us of illusions and demand presence. In such moments, many feel broken. But perhaps what is breaking is not the self—but the shell that kept the soul hidden.

Do not rush to escape pain. Sit with it. Listen to what it is asking you to remember. The soul is never absent in suffering—it is most visible there. Like a candle in a dark room, its glow becomes unmistakable in silence and sorrow.

Living Soulfully

To live soulfully means to live with awareness, depth, and integrity. It means:

- Speaking only what aligns with your truth.
- Doing work that lights you from within.
- Creating space for joy, rest, and reflection.
- Serving not from guilt, but from fullness.
- Saying no when your spirit feels heavy.
- Saying yes when your heart feels open.

The soul seeks authenticity, not perfection. You are not here to perform life—you are here to live it fully, in alignment with who you truly are.

Conclusion: The Soul is Your Forever Companion

In the end, titles fade. Relationships evolve. The body ages. But the soul? It stays. It was with you before your first breath, and it will be with you beyond your last. The soul is not a mystery to be solved; it is a presence to be felt. And its whisper will never lead you astray.

So be still. Be honest. Be brave.

The soul is speaking.

Are you ready to listen?

FOUR
WHY WE ABANDON OURSELVES

"The tragedy of life is not that we die. The tragedy is that somewhere along the way, we forget who we truly are."

Introduction: The Quiet Tragedy

Self-abandonment is one of the quietest and most painful tragedies of human life. Unlike heartbreak or loss, it doesn't arrive with noise. It creeps in gently—sometimes as compromise, sometimes as fear, often as the desperate need to belong. It starts with silencing your own needs to avoid conflict, then grows into living a life shaped by others' expectations. Before long, you become a stranger to yourself.

The soul whispers, "Stay close to me." But the world pulls, persuades, and pressures you to move away.

Why do we walk away from our own essence? Why do we mute the voice inside that once spoke so clearly? The answers are not simple. They lie buried under layers of childhood conditioning, societal norms, and wounds we often do not realize we carry.

This chapter explores how and why we abandon ourselves—so that we may begin the sacred journey of returning home.

The Innocence We Once Knew

We were not born disconnected.

As children, we were deeply attuned to our emotions and instincts. We cried when we were hungry, laughed when something delighted us, and recoiled when something felt unsafe. We were unapologetically ourselves. The soul and body moved in harmony, expressing what was true moment to moment.

But slowly, the world began to teach us otherwise.

You may remember the first time someone told you not to cry. Or when your excitement was met with scolding. Perhaps you were called "too sensitive," "too wild," or "too much." These weren't just words. They were messages: **Who you are is not acceptable. You must become someone else.**

This is where the self begins to fracture.

We learned that love could be withdrawn. That attention was conditional. That to survive in a family, in a classroom, in a society—we had to adapt. And so, we did.

We became the obedient child, the achiever, the peacemaker, the strong one. We wore these roles so well, we forgot we were wearing masks at all.

This is the beginning of self-abandonment: the gradual rejection of who we truly are in exchange for who the world wants us to be.

Childhood Conditioning: The Blueprint of Disconnection

Children are like sponges. They absorb not only the words spoken to them but also the unspoken energy of their environment. If love was inconsistent, they may internalize the belief, *I must be unlovable.* If they were punished for expressing anger, they learn to suppress it—burying it deep in the body.

Common messages children receive, consciously or unconsciously:

- "Be quiet."
- "Don't be a burden."
- "Stop crying or I'll give you something to cry about."
- "Good boys/girls don't do that."
- "You're being dramatic."
- "You're not trying hard enough."

Such messages do not merely guide behaviour. They shape identity.

Eventually, the child starts asking:

What parts of me are allowed? What parts must I hide to be safe, loved, and accepted?

This creates an internal hierarchy of self. The "acceptable" traits rise to the surface, while the "unacceptable" ones are banished to the shadows. Joy becomes quiet. Anger becomes shame. Dreams are put away like toys we're told we've outgrown.

Society's Mold: The Great Standardization

As we grow older, society takes over where the family left off. Schools reward conformity and obedience more than creativity or emotional intelligence. Media shows us who is worthy: those who are beautiful, successful, productive, popular. Culture tells us what is desirable and what is not. It offers us an image of the "ideal self"—polished, performative, and detached from vulnerability.

You learn quickly that certain dreams are "unrealistic," that rest is laziness, that pain is weakness. And so, you start chasing what the world rewards, even if it doesn't nourish you. You choose careers for prestige, partners for appearance, goals for validation. But no matter how much you achieve, something feels off. Empty. Distant.

Because you left yourself behind.

To meet societal standards, we often amputate the wildest, most magical parts of ourselves. We become efficient, competent, admired—but hollow.

This is not because we are flawed. It is because we were taught to value performance over presence, appearance over authenticity.

Trauma: The Silent Divider

Trauma is not always a dramatic event. Sometimes, it is a series of small moments where you needed comfort but received silence, where you needed protection but felt alone.

Trauma tells us, *it is not safe to be me.*

Whether it was bullying, neglect, emotional abuse, or the absence of attunement, trauma fractures the bond between self and soul. We begin to distrust our instincts, ignore our needs, and dissociate from our bodies. We float through life, functioning but unfeeling.

To survive trauma, many of us disconnect from ourselves. We build armour. We become what others need us to be. But this survival strategy comes at a price: we lose access to our own inner truth.

The tragedy is not only in what happened—but in the way it taught us to disappear from our own lives.

The Many Faces of Self-Abandonment

Self-abandonment doesn't always look dramatic. Often, it appears in daily choices:

- Saying yes when you mean no.
- Dismissing your emotions as "too much."
- Staying in draining relationships out of guilt.
- Silencing your truth to avoid disapproval.
- Seeking constant external validation.
- Neglecting rest, nourishment, and care.
- Distracting yourself from pain rather than feeling it.

Every time you dismiss your needs; you teach yourself that you are not worth showing up for.

Over time, this disconnection becomes normal. You no longer ask yourself what you want, what you feel, what you need. You exist on autopilot—efficient but exhausted, surrounded yet lonely, achieving but unfulfilled.

The body begins to ache. The soul begins to whisper. But you don't understand the language anymore.

Why We Continue the Pattern

Even as adults, with full awareness of our pain, we continue to abandon ourselves. Why?

Because returning to the self can feel terrifying. It means facing the grief of what we've lost, the shame of who we've become, the wounds we've buried. It means risking rejection, making different choices, and disappointing people who benefit from our silence.

Most of all, it means unlearning everything we were taught about who we are.

There is safety in familiarity—even if that familiarity is painful. Many of us prefer the discomfort we know to the unknown healing that awaits. The cage may be small, but it is predictable. The open field? It is uncertain.

But until we are willing to face the discomfort of truth, we will remain in cycles of self-betrayal.

The Cost of Abandoning the Self

Self-abandonment has a price. It may not be immediate, but it accumulates.

- Emotional numbness.
- Chronic anxiety or depression.
- Unfulfilling relationships.
- Addictions and compulsions.
- Creative blocks.
- A persistent sense of meaninglessness.

The greatest cost is that you live a life that is not truly yours.

And even if you succeed by the world's standards, the soul knows the difference. It longs not for perfection, but for authenticity. It does not care how impressive you look. It only wants to be known by you.

The First Step Back: Awareness

Healing begins with awareness.

To reclaim yourself, you must first acknowledge where and how you left. Not with shame—but with compassion. Self-abandonment is not your fault. It was a survival strategy. A wise adaptation. But now, it is time to choose differently.

Begin asking:

- Where do I silence my truth to feel safe?
- Whose approval am I still chasing?
- What parts of me have I rejected?

• What did I need as a child that I didn't receive?

Awareness is painful, yes—but it is the birth of freedom.

Honouring the Inner World

To stop abandoning yourself, you must begin to honour your inner world.

This means:

• Trusting your emotions as valid.
• Listening to your body's signals.
• Giving space to your desires.
• Speaking your truth, even if your voice shakes.
• Holding yourself through pain with tenderness.
• Restoring the broken bond with your own heart.

This is not a one-time act. It is a daily practice of returning—to your breath, your body, your boundaries, your joy.

Becoming Your Own Home Again

Imagine this:

You are no longer a stranger to your own soul. You wake with clarity, speak with integrity, rest without guilt. You no longer ask the world for permission to be whole. You remember your worth—not because someone told you, but because you reclaimed it.

This is the power of coming home to yourself.

Yes, the world may resist. Some may call you selfish. But let them. Choosing yourself is not betrayal. It is restoration.

When you no longer abandon yourself, you model for others what it means to live in truth. You become a light—not because you shine for others, but because you refused to extinguish your own flame.

Closing Reflection

We abandoned ourselves not out of weakness, but out of need. We did it to survive.

But now, survival is not enough. We are called to thrive, to remember, to return.

You owe no one your silence, your exhaustion, your conformity. You owe yourself your own loyalty. And it is never too late to begin again.

The child you once were is still waiting. The soul you forgot still whispers. The body still longs to be heard.

You are not lost. You are just one honest breath away from coming home.

FIVE

THE MYTH OF LONELINESS

"You are never alone. Your breath is with you. Your heartbeat is with you. Your soul has never once left your side."

The Illusion of Emptiness

Loneliness is a word that echoes with sorrow in the hollow corridors of the human heart. It whispers of separation, abandonment, and the cold ache of being unseen. We have all felt it—on a crowded street, at a dinner table with friends, even in the arms of someone we love. It wears many faces. Yet, what if loneliness is not what we think it is? What if it is not an absence, but a doorway?

We live in a world that prizes connection but often misunderstands it. Social media promises closeness through likes and messages, yet leaves many feeling more isolated. We are surrounded by noise, yet starved for presence. This is not true loneliness. This is disconnection from self. The myth of loneliness begins the moment we forget that our greatest companionship has always been within.

The Body as a Constant Companion

Your body is not a shell you inhabit. It is a faithful companion, a sacred partner, a living witness to your journey. From your first breath to your last, it has held you, fought for you, healed you. When others left, it stayed. When you felt lost, it carried you. It stores every joy, every pain, every whisper of your lived experience.

We rarely listen to the body until it aches. We treat it like a machine—expecting it to perform, to endure, to keep going. But your body is not machinery. It is sentient. It feels. It remembers. It weeps and rejoices in its own language.

The next time you feel alone, place a hand over your heart. Feel the rhythm. That is not just a heartbeat. That is the presence of life itself, pulsing with devotion. You have never truly been alone, because your body has always been here, waiting to be acknowledged, held, and thanked.

The Soul: Your Silent Witness

If the body is your earthly companion, the soul is your eternal one. It existed before words, before thought, before form. It knows your true name—not the one given by parents, not the one used by the world, but the one that speaks of your essence.

When you cry without knowing why, when you feel peace in a forest or hear truth in a stranger's voice—that is the soul speaking. It has never judged you. Never left you. Even when you turned away, it stood by.

Many feel lonely because they have forgotten how to hear the soul. They chase validation, yearn for belonging, seek love in all the places that echo back their own disconnection. But the soul waits patiently. It speaks in dreams, in synchronicities, in sudden insights. It does not scream. It sings.

To remember the soul is to remember that you are never alone. You are witnessed by something deeper than eyes, known by something older than memory.

The Cultural Obsession with Togetherness

Society worships external companionship. We are told to find our "other half," as though we are incomplete. We are taught that to be alone is to be lacking, pitied, avoided. Solitude is painted as something tragic, or something to be filled with noise and distraction.

But what if solitude is sacred?

The mystics knew this. They sought the mountains, the deserts, the caves. Not to escape life, but to encounter it more fully. They understood that aloneness is not the absence of connection, but its deepest form. It is here, in silence, that we meet the Divine. It is here that we learn to listen again.

The modern world fears this silence. We fill it with entertainment, conversation, plans. But in doing so, we miss the profound gift of our own presence. True solitude is not a lack. It is a richness that cannot be bought or performed.

Loneliness vs. Aloneness

It is essential to distinguish loneliness from aloneness.

Loneliness is the belief that no one sees or understands you. Aloneness is the experience of being with yourself fully.

Loneliness feels like exile. Aloneness feels like return.

When you are lonely, you crave someone else to complete your sentence, to reflect your worth. When you are truly alone, you complete your own thoughts and discover your intrinsic value.

This does not mean we don't need each other. We do. We are relational beings. But our relationships become richer when we no longer enter them out of emptiness. When we no longer demand from others what we have not yet given ourselves.

The Inner Dialogue

One of the most powerful practices to dismantle the myth of loneliness is conscious inner dialogue. To speak to yourself with love, curiosity, and respect.

Try this: Sit quietly. Breathe. And ask within, "How am I feeling right now?" Wait for an answer. It may come as a word, a sensation, an image. Respond with kindness. Like you would to a dear friend.

This simple practice can begin to restore the bond between self and soul. It transforms loneliness into intimacy. The more you commune with your inner world, the less desperate you become for outer approval. And paradoxically, this makes your outer relationships more genuine, because they are not built on need, but on mutual presence.

Nature: The Great Companion

When human connection feels distant, nature offers companionship that asks for nothing but your presence. A tree will never judge you. A river will never abandon you. The stars do not care about your resume.

To walk in nature is to walk among ancient friends. Trees hold the memories of wind and time. Birds sing without agenda. The sky embraces you, whether you smile or cry.

Many who feel alone find solace among the wild because nature mirrors back their own aliveness. It whispers, "You belong here. You are not separate. You are part of this vast, breathing world."

Dreams, Symbols, and the Unseen

There are worlds within you that you have yet to visit. Dreams, symbols, and metaphors arise from these realms. They are the soul's language. Every dream is a message. Every intuitive nudge, a guide.

We often ignore these signs because they do not speak in linear logic. But they are proof that you are never truly alone. Something within is always communicating. Always guiding. Always reaching toward wholeness.

Start keeping a dream journal. Listen to the feelings behind the symbols. Treat your inner life as a sacred text. You will begin to see how rich, mysterious, and connected your existence truly is.

Reclaiming Sacred Solitude

To transform the myth of loneliness, we must reclaim solitude as sacred. This is not the same as isolation, which is rooted in fear. Sacred solitude is chosen, honoured, and nourished.

Make space each day to be with yourself. Not to do, but to be. Light a candle. Sit in silence. Let the thoughts come and go like clouds. Listen not for answers, but for presence.

In this quiet, you will feel the warmth of your own essence. You will remember that the soul does not shout. It whispers. And it has been whispering all along: "You are not alone. I am here."

From Separation to Belonging

The journey from loneliness to belonging is not about finding more people. It is about remembering the unbreakable connection to yourself, to the Earth, to the unseen world.

You were never dropped here alone. You were woven into existence. The air you breathe, the ground beneath your feet, the silence in your heart—all of it is companionship.

You belong. Not because you earned it. Not because others say so. But because you are.

Closing Reflection

Loneliness is not an enemy. It is a messenger. It tells you that you have wandered far from your inner hearth. It asks you to return, not in shame, but in reverence.

You are not alone. You have never been. Your body listens. Your soul remembers. The world awaits your presence. Let the myth dissolve. Let truth return.

Let this be the beginning of sacred companionship with the one person who will never leave you: **yourself.**

SIX

NUMBING THE BODY, SILENCING THE SOUL

In the quiet moments between tasks, when the noise of the world fades, something ancient within us stirs. A discomfort, subtle and persistent, rises—not loud enough to alarm, but enough to seek relief. For many, this is the moment where we reach for our phones, pour another drink, turn on a screen, or immerse ourselves in yet another task. These acts seem harmless, even productive or relaxing. Yet beneath the surface, they represent a tragic pact: the choice to numb the body and silence the soul.

The Subtle Art of Escape

We live in a culture that teaches us to escape our inner life rather than explore it. Pain, sadness, fear, boredom—these are not merely discouraged emotions; they are pathologized. We are trained to move quickly past them, to find distraction, pleasure, or productivity as a substitute for presence. As a result, we become fluent in avoidance, skilled in suppression.

This escape can take many forms. Some numb with substances—alcohol, drugs, sugar, caffeine. Others with behaviours—compulsive scrolling, overworking, obsessive organizing, constant talking. Even healthy practices like exercise or dieting can become tools of escape if used to avoid listening to what the body and soul are trying to say.

In this way, we unknowingly declare war on our own being. We train ourselves to mute the signals of the body—fatigue, tension, hunger, desire—and disregard the whispers of the soul—intuition, longing, grief, creativity. What we call modern life is, in many ways, a prolonged performance of avoidance.

The Cost of Disconnection

But there is always a cost. The more we numb, the more we distance ourselves from what is real. The body begins to ache in confusion, burdened by the weight of emotions not felt and needs not met. The soul recedes into quiet corners, waiting to be heard, watching as we trade aliveness for temporary comfort.

This disconnection manifests in countless ways: insomnia, anxiety, unexplained sadness, chronic fatigue, a sense of meaninglessness. These are not defects but signals—calls from within asking us to stop running. They are the body and soul pleading for acknowledgment.

When we silence these cries, we risk forgetting who we are. We become shells, functioning but not thriving. Existing but not truly living. The world may see us as successful or happy, but inwardly we know something essential has been lost.

Addiction as Misunderstood Longing

Addiction, in all its forms, is not simply a failure of will or morality—it is, at its core, a response to unmet inner need. It is the soul's desperate attempt to feel something—anything—that resembles connection. The drink, the pill, the purchase, the gamble—each is a distorted gesture toward wholeness.

Rather than judging these behaviours, we must approach them with compassion. To ask: What pain is this numbing? What voice is being silenced? What truth am I not ready to face? These are not easy questions. They require courage. But only through them can healing begin.

True freedom does not come from denying our impulses, but from understanding them. We must sit with our discomfort long enough to hear what it has to say. We must be willing to feel the pain we've spent a lifetime avoiding. Only then can we begin to reclaim our inner life.

Overwork: The Mask of Worthiness

In many societies, overwork is not just tolerated—it is celebrated. Productivity becomes synonymous with value. To be busy is to be important. But beneath this cultural applause lies a deep spiritual crisis. Many of us work ourselves to exhaustion not because we love what we do, but because we are afraid of who we are without it.

When we stop working, what remains? Silence. Stillness. The haunting question: Am I enough? For those disconnected from their body and soul, the answer often feels like no. So we keep moving, keep achieving, keep proving our worth.

This form of numbing is particularly insidious because it hides behind the guise of responsibility. Yet it robs us of rest, of presence, of joy. Our bodies break down. Our souls grow weary. And still we keep going, afraid of what might surface if we stop.

Distraction: The Noise That Drowns the Inner Voice

We live in an age of endless distraction. Our phones, our feeds, our notifications—all designed to keep us stimulated, reactive, engaged. But engagement is not the same as connection. In fact, the more externally engaged we are, the less internally connected we often become.

Distraction is not neutral. It takes energy. It steals focus. And it silences the subtle voice within. The soul does not shout; it whispers. It speaks in quiet nudges, strange dreams, sudden tears. It waits for us to turn inward. But in a world that rewards speed and stimulation, the soul is easily ignored.

When we finally unplug, we may find ourselves anxious, restless, even afraid. This is not a flaw; it is a detox. It is the return of what has long been suppressed. It is the beginning of reconnection.

Listening as Radical Practice

To reverse the numbing process, we must begin to listen—not casually, but with sacred attention. This means slowing down. It means creating moments of stillness where the body can be felt and the soul can speak.

Ask yourself gently: What am I feeling right now, in my body? What sensations are present? What emotions arise when I sit in silence? What is my soul longing for?

You do not need immediate answers. The act of asking is itself an opening. Over time, with patience and practice, the body will begin to trust you again. The soul will begin to share its truth.

You may cry for no reason. You may remember a buried memory. You may feel tired, or angry, or alive. All of this is welcome. All of it is real.

Returning to Wholeness

To be whole is not to be perfect. It is to be present. It is to allow all parts of ourselves—the pain, the joy, the confusion, the desire—to be seen and held. It is to stop running and start witnessing.

This journey requires tenderness. It requires forgiveness—for the ways we've abandoned ourselves, the ways we've coped. We must thank the distractions, the addictions, the busyness—for they were, in their own way, attempts to survive. And then we must release them.

Wholeness comes not from addition, but from subtraction. Removing the noise. Releasing the false roles. Remembering the truth of who we are beneath it all.

The Courage to Feel

Perhaps the bravest act in this world is to feel. To feel the body, with all its aches and pleasures. To feel the soul, with all its mystery and longing. To allow the inner world to be known and honoured.

This is not always comfortable. But it is the path to true freedom. The path to love—not the fleeting kind that depends on others, but the enduring kind that arises from within.

When you feel the fullness of your own being, you no longer need to numb. You no longer fear the silence. Because in that silence, you discover that you were never alone. Your body was always speaking. Your soul was always whispering. You only needed to listen.

Final Reflections

You are not broken. You are not weak. You are a living, breathing testament to resilience. You have endured, survived, adapted. But now, the invitation is to return—not to who you were, but to who you've always been.

This chapter is not about blaming yourself for how you've coped. It is about reclaiming your right to feel, to rest, to listen, to be whole. It is a call to come home—to your body, your soul, your sacred self.

Let this be the beginning of your return. Let the numbing end here. Let the silence be filled not with noise, but with presence. Let the voice of your body and the whisper of your soul guide you forward.

They have been waiting all along.

SEVEN

THE LANGUAGE OF FATIGUE AND PAIN

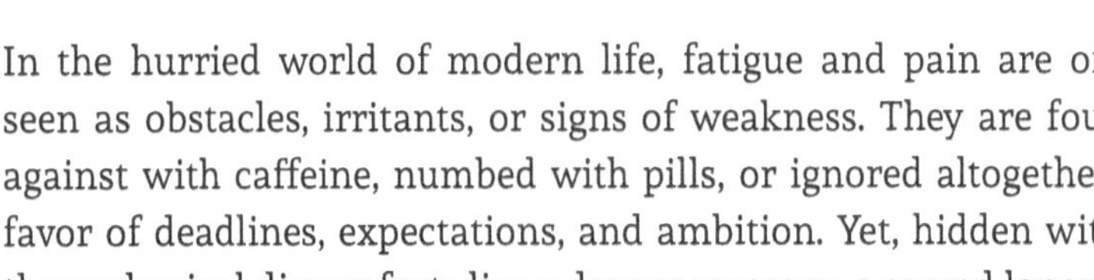

In the hurried world of modern life, fatigue and pain are often seen as obstacles, irritants, or signs of weakness. They are fought against with caffeine, numbed with pills, or ignored altogether in favor of deadlines, expectations, and ambition. Yet, hidden within these physical discomforts lies a deeper message, a sacred language that the body speaks with utmost sincerity. To truly understand ourselves, we must learn to listen to the messages embedded within fatigue and pain—messages that are often the body's plea for compassion, rest, and awareness.

The Body as a Messenger

The body does not lie. It cannot fabricate a narrative or create falsehoods like the mind can. It responds, reflects, and reacts in real-time. When fatigue settles into your limbs or pain flares in a muscle or joint, it is not an act of betrayal—it is a sign, a message written in the ancient language of biology and being. This language is neither cruel nor punitive; it is protective, compassionate, and deeply wise.

Pain tells us that something is wrong. Fatigue tells us that something is depleted. The body is asking for recalibration. Yet, rather than meeting these messages with curiosity, we are trained to fight, suppress, or override them. In doing so, we silence our most loyal companion and drift further from the alignment that our soul seeks.

Fatigue: The Body's Whisper of Overextension

Fatigue is more than physical tiredness. It can be emotional, mental, or spiritual. It arrives when the body and soul are stretched beyond their capacity, often without rest, nourishment, or acknowledgment. Modern culture glorifies burnout, equating productivity with worthiness. But when the body begins to feel heavy, when concentration falters and sleep becomes elusive or insufficient, the body is not failing—it is begging for balance.

Philosophically, fatigue is the embodiment of forgotten boundaries. It is the shadow of self-neglect. It speaks not only to our daily actions but to the deeper, unconscious contracts we have made with a society that values doing over being.

Fatigue invites us to pause. To step away. To reflect. It asks the soul to return to stillness and the body to be held in care. It is not weakness; it is wisdom.

Pain: The Sacred Alarm

Pain, though often dreaded, is sacred. It sharpens our attention. It anchors us in the present. It reminds us that we are alive, vulnerable, and in need of tending.

Pain is not just physical—it can reside in the gut, in the heart, in the silent weeping of the spirit. Chronic pain especially is a call not just for medical attention but for deep inner inquiry. Where are we misaligned? What parts of ourselves have we disowned? What truth have we swallowed or denied?

In a philosophical sense, pain is the body's poetry. It forces the ego to surrender. It cracks open the illusion of control and forces humility. To be in pain is to confront the raw edge of existence, to sit with the reality that all things are impermanent and that healing requires attention, not denial.

The Cumulative Cost of Ignoring

Each time we ignore fatigue, we place another weight upon our spirit. Each time we numb pain instead of listening to it, we distance ourselves from the sacred dialogue between body and soul. Over time, these ignored whispers become screams. Chronic illness, burnout, depression, and disconnection are often not random—they are the cumulative result of silencing the body's language.

We are not machines. We are symphonies of muscle, bone, emotion, and spirit. When one instrument plays too loud for too long, the harmony collapses. Restoring that harmony requires tuning in, listening closely, and responding with reverence.

Learning to Listen Again

To understand the language of fatigue and pain, we must cultivate stillness. This begins with presence. Before reaching for distraction or remedy, ask the body: What are you trying to tell me?

Rest your hand where it hurts. Breathe into the space of exhaustion. Speak kindly to yourself. "I hear you. I'm here." This simple act of turning inward reestablishes the bond that we so often lose in the chase for external validation.

Journaling, breathwork, meditation, somatic therapy—these are not luxuries, but essential tools in translating the body's language. They bring clarity to the murky waters of sensation and guide us back to ourselves.

Rewriting the Narrative

Instead of framing pain as a problem, frame it as a message. Instead of seeing fatigue as failure, see it as feedback. This shift in perception is not merely psychological—it is spiritual. It is the reawakening of a partnership that has always existed but has been buried beneath layers of expectation and noise.

In ancient traditions, pain was seen as a rite of passage, a teacher. The ache of the body was a threshold into deeper awareness. Whether it was the monk sitting in silent meditation, the pilgrim walking vast distances, or the healer confronting their own illness—each recognized pain not as an enemy but as a companion on the path to wholeness.

Honouring the Body's Limits

To honour your body is to recognize its limits—not as constraints but as sacred boundaries. When the body says "no," it is not being lazy or uncooperative. It is protecting you. When it craves rest, solitude, or nourishment, it is not being indulgent—it is restoring your capacity to love, create, and serve.

We live in a culture that praises pushing through. But there is quiet heroism in slowing down, in saying, "Enough for now." There is courage in resting. There is strength in softness.

Integration: From Message to Meaning

Once we learn to listen, the next step is integration. What does the fatigue reveal about our lifestyle, our priorities, our unspoken wounds? What does pain show us about unresolved trauma, repressed emotion, or the need for transformation?

Integration is the act of making meaning from the message. It is where philosophy meets practice. It's where we stop treating the body as an inconvenience and begin treating it as a sacred compass. This process is ongoing. As we age, evolve, and grow, the messages change. But the language remains, always waiting to be understood.

Final Reflections

Your body is not the enemy. It is not a vessel to conquer, a machine to exploit, or a problem to solve. It is your first and last home, the keeper of your memories, the witness of your life.

Fatigue is the sigh of your body saying, "Please, be gentle." Pain is the alarm saying, "Please, pay attention." When we turn toward these signals with curiosity instead of contempt, we reclaim a sacred intimacy with ourselves.

In this intimacy, loneliness fades. In this listening, healing begins. And in this union, the body and soul speak together, reminding you that you are not broken—you are simply being called back home.

Practice for the Chapter:

Take 10 minutes each evening to sit quietly and scan your body from head to toe. Notice areas of tightness, heat, ache, or fatigue. Instead of labelling or judging, simply place your awareness there and breathe. Ask gently, "What do you need from me?" Write down the answers that arise, even if they are unclear at first. Over time, you'll learn to trust the language of your own body.

This is the beginning of deep self-communion. This is how the healing begins.

EIGHT

THE SOUL'S LONGING FOR ATTENTION

In the quiet moments between breaths, when the mind settles and the noise of the world fades, there emerges a subtle sensation: a deep, unspoken yearning. It may manifest as restlessness, a vague emptiness, or an incessant longing that no external pleasure or achievement seems to satisfy. This feeling, though often misunderstood, is the soul's cry for attention — a plea from the deepest part of our being that has been neglected or ignored for far too long.

The Invisible Presence Within

The soul is often described as the essence of who we are — that invisible, intangible core that transcends the body and mind. Unlike the physical form, it does not make its presence known through obvious gestures or loud proclamations. Instead, it whispers, nudges, and sometimes shouts in the silence of our inner world. Yet, in a society that prizes action, speed, and distraction, the language of the soul is frequently drowned out by the clamour of external demands.

When we neglect this inner voice, the soul does not disappear; it becomes restless. It stirs beneath the surface, sending signals that may be disguised as anxiety, dissatisfaction, or a sense of aimlessness. This restlessness is not a flaw but a sacred message — a sign that the soul is awake, waiting for us to listen.

Restlessness as a Call to Reconnection

Restlessness often feels uncomfortable, even painful. It can make us feel like we are caught in an endless loop of dissatisfaction, chasing goals that never quite bring fulfilment. But what if this restlessness is actually a compass, pointing us back to ourselves?

Philosophically, restlessness can be seen as the soul's way of breaking through the numbness created by routine and distraction. It is the longing for a deeper connection — not just with the world around us, but with the inner realm of meaning, purpose, and authenticity. It urges us to pause and ask: What parts of me have been silenced? What truths have I yet to acknowledge?

Emptiness: The Shadow of Disconnection

Emptiness is another common experience that stems from the soul's longing. Unlike physical hunger, this emptiness cannot be filled with food, possessions, or accomplishments. It is a spiritual void, a silent ache that no amount of external stimulation can satiate.

This emptiness arises when we have lost touch with our authentic selves. It is the shadow cast by disconnection — disconnection from our values, passions, relationships, and ultimately, from the soul itself. It serves as a mirror, reflecting the need for healing and realignment.

Yearning: The Soul's Invitation

Yearning is perhaps the most profound expression of the soul's desire for attention. It is a deep, often ineffable feeling that transcends specific wants or needs. Unlike restlessness or emptiness, yearning carries a quality of sacredness — a silent invitation to explore the unknown depths within.

This yearning can inspire transformation. It can lead us to seek meaning beyond material success, to cultivate compassion, creativity, and spiritual growth. It beckons us to embrace the mystery of existence and our unique place within it.

The Roots of the Soul's Neglect

Understanding why the soul's voice becomes unheard requires examining the forces that pull us away from inner awareness. Childhood conditioning, cultural expectations, trauma, and the relentless pace of modern life all contribute to the suppression of the soul's language.

From a young age, many are taught to prioritize external validation over internal truth. We learn to conform, to silence our doubts and dreams in favour of social acceptance. Over time, this pattern leads to a gradual erosion of the soul's presence, replaced by a persona designed to survive rather than thrive.

The Price of Ignoring the Soul

Ignoring the soul's longing has profound consequences. It manifests as emotional distress, chronic dissatisfaction, and a pervasive sense of meaninglessness. The more we turn away from the soul, the louder its call becomes, sometimes erupting in crises that force us to confront what we have long avoided.

Philosophically, this process is part of the human journey. The soul's restlessness is a catalyst for growth, urging us to awaken from unconscious living and embrace a fuller, richer existence.

Listening to the Soul's Language

Learning to hear the soul requires cultivating stillness and presence. Meditation, reflection, and creative expression are powerful tools that open channels to the inner world. In these practices, we begin to recognize the subtle signals — a feeling, an image, a spontaneous insight — that convey the soul's messages.

The soul's language is poetic and symbolic, often revealing itself in dreams, intuition, and moments of profound beauty. It speaks through the body's sensations and emotions, reminding us that the spiritual and physical are intimately intertwined.

Responding to the Soul's Call

Attention is the soul's nourishment. When we respond to its longing, we nurture our wholeness and foster a sense of harmony between body, mind, and spirit. This response takes many forms — setting boundaries, pursuing passions, cultivating meaningful relationships, and engaging in practices that honour our deepest values.

Philosophically, responding to the soul is an act of courage and authenticity. It requires shedding masks and facing the unknown aspects of ourselves with compassion and curiosity.

The Journey Toward Wholeness

The soul's longing is not a problem to be fixed but a journey to be embraced. It invites us to explore the depths of our being, to integrate the light and shadow within, and to live with greater presence and purpose.

This journey is ongoing and ever-evolving. As we listen and respond, the soul's restlessness transforms into peace, emptiness fills with meaning, and yearning blossoms into fulfilment.

Final Reflections

Your soul is a sacred companion on the path of life, patiently waiting for your attention. Restlessness, emptiness, and yearning are not signs of failure but invitations to deeper awareness.

By embracing the soul's longing, you embark on a transformative journey toward self-discovery and healing. In this sacred dialogue between your inner and outer worlds, you find not only yourself but the profound interconnectedness of all existence.

Practice for the Chapter:

Set aside quiet time daily to reflect on moments of restlessness or emptiness. Journal your feelings without judgment and ask yourself: What is my soul trying to tell me? Over time, cultivate practices — such as meditation, art, or nature walks — that deepen your connection with this inner voice.

This is the path to listening, healing, and awakening the soul's timeless wisdom.

NINE

RECONNECTING THROUGH STILLNESS

In a world overflowing with noise, distraction, and ceaseless activity, stillness often feels like an elusive luxury. Yet it is precisely within stillness that the most profound reconnection with ourselves—the reunion of body and soul—can take place. This chapter explores how meditation, silence, and mindful awareness serve as essential pathways to rediscovering the companionship that has always been present within us, waiting patiently beneath the surface of our hurried lives.

The Paradox of Stillness in Motion

At first glance, stillness appears passive, a state of doing nothing. But philosophically, stillness is anything but inactivity. It is an active state of presence, an open invitation to listen deeply—to our body's sensations, to the soul's whispers, and to the silent language of being itself.

Stillness is the ground from which awareness arises. It is the fertile soil where the seeds of self-understanding, healing, and transformation take root. When we cultivate stillness, we pause the relentless flow of thoughts and distractions long enough to witness the richness of our inner world. In this pause, the fragmented pieces of our experience begin to coalesce into a coherent whole.

The Body in Stillness: A Living Temple

Our body is often overlooked or undervalued as a mere vessel for the mind or spirit. Yet, in stillness, the body reveals itself as a living temple—a sacred space that holds the entirety of our experience.

When we slow down, we become more attuned to bodily sensations—heartbeat, breath, muscle tension, or relaxation. These sensations are not random; they are messages and reflections of our inner state. By bringing mindful awareness to the body, we deepen our connection with the present moment and with the reality of being alive.

The practice of stillness allows the body to relax its habitual defenses—muscle tightness, rapid breathing, and tension—opening pathways for emotional release and healing. It teaches us to trust the wisdom held within our physical form and to honour its needs with kindness and compassion.

The Soul's Voice Emerges in Silence

If the body is a temple, silence is its sacred sanctuary. In silence, the soul's language becomes more audible. The clamouring demands of the outside world quiet, allowing us to hear the subtle currents of intuition, inspiration, and inner knowing.

Philosophically, silence is not emptiness but fullness. It is a rich, fertile presence that holds all possibilities. It transcends words and concepts, connecting us with the infinite mystery of existence. In this profound silence, the soul speaks not through words but through feeling, symbols, and presence.

Regularly entering into silence—whether through meditation, contemplative prayer, or quiet solitude—creates space for the soul to express its deepest longings, wisdom, and guidance. It becomes a sacred dialogue, a communion between the finite self and the boundless inner being.

Mindful Awareness: The Art of Being Present

Stillness alone is not enough if the mind remains scattered or distracted. Mindful awareness is the skilful attention that brings focus to the present moment without judgment or resistance.

Mindfulness trains us to observe thoughts, feelings, and sensations as passing phenomena rather than fixed realities. It breaks the habitual patterns of rumination, worry, and identification with fleeting mental states.

By cultivating mindful awareness, we become witnesses to our inner landscape, able to respond with clarity rather than react impulsively. This clarity fosters a harmonious relationship between body and soul, allowing them to move together in grace and balance.

Meditation: A Bridge to Inner Companionship

Meditation is one of the most accessible and transformative practices for cultivating stillness and mindful awareness. It is a disciplined approach to training the mind and opening the heart.

There are many forms of meditation—focused attention, open awareness, loving-kindness, guided visualization—each offering unique ways to connect deeply with ourselves. The common thread among these practices is the invitation to turn inward, to rest in presence, and to gently observe whatever arises.

Through meditation, the boundaries between body, mind, and soul soften. We learn to embrace the entirety of our experience with acceptance, compassion, and curiosity. The meditative state nurtures self-companionship, where the body and soul become trusted friends rather than strangers or adversaries.

The Challenge of Stillness in a Busy World

Despite the clear benefits, stillness can be intimidating or uncomfortable for many. The silence may bring up buried emotions or unresolved conflicts. The mind may resist by generating restlessness or boredom.

These challenges are part of the process. They reveal the layers of avoidance and distraction that have kept us separated from our true nature. Facing them with patience and kindness is itself a practice in self-love and healing.

Moreover, integrating stillness into daily life requires intention and consistency. Even brief moments—pausing to breathe deeply, observing sensations while washing dishes, or sitting quietly before sleep—can build the habit of mindful presence.

The Ripple Effects of Reconnection

When we cultivate stillness and reconnect with our body and soul, the effects ripple outward. Our relationships deepen as we become more present and authentic. Our work gains meaning as it aligns with inner values. Our resilience strengthens, allowing us to navigate life's challenges with equanimity.

Philosophically, this reconnection is a return to our essential nature—whole, interconnected, and alive. It dissolves the illusion of separation and invites us into a lived experience of unity and peace.

Embracing Stillness as a Daily Practice

The path to reconnection through stillness is not a one-time event but a lifelong journey. It calls for dedication and gentleness, an ongoing commitment to honour the sacred companionship of body and soul.

Simple daily practices can anchor us in stillness:

- Begin each day with mindful breathing or meditation.
- Take intentional pauses throughout the day to check in with bodily sensations.
- Spend time in nature, letting its quiet presence inspire inner calm.
- Practice gratitude for the living presence within you.
- Create a ritual space—a corner for meditation, journaling, or silent reflection.

These practices build a sanctuary within, a refuge where the soul's voice can be heard clearly and the body's wisdom honoured.

Conclusion: The Gift of Stillness

Stillness is the doorway to a profound companionship that transcends external circumstances. It reveals the enduring friendship between body and soul, a bond that remains steady even when life feels chaotic or uncertain.

By embracing stillness, we open ourselves to a deeper awareness and a richer experience of being. In this sacred space, we find the essence of true self-care—a loving presence that listens, heals, and transforms.

Practice for the Chapter:

Set aside ten to twenty minutes daily to sit in silence. Focus on your breath or bodily sensations without trying to change anything. When thoughts arise, acknowledge them gently and return to your point of focus. Over time, notice how this practice deepens your connection with your inner self.

TEN

THE FIRST PACT: I AM WITH ME

The most vital relationship is often the one we neglect—our relationship with ourselves. Amid the complex rhythms of life, where duties, expectations, and connections tug us in every direction, it's easy to lose sight of nurturing our inner world. This chapter invites you to make a solemn pact, a heartfelt commitment to yourself: *I am with me.* This is not a fleeting promise but a foundational alliance, a declaration that you will show up for yourself as your own best friend, guardian, and companion.

The Importance of the Inner Covenant

Why is it necessary to consciously commit to being with yourself? The answer lies in the nature of all relationships: every connection we have externally is ultimately filtered through the relationship we have within. When we harbour judgment, neglect, or indifference toward ourselves, those feelings ripple outward, shaping how we engage with others and the world.

A pact with yourself anchors you in self-trust and self-respect. It is a profound recognition that, despite the uncertainty and change swirling around you, there is one presence that will never abandon you—your own being, composed of body and soul. This alliance becomes a sanctuary where you can find refuge, guidance, and unconditional support.

Philosophically, this pact is an act of sovereignty. It is the moment you reclaim your power—not by controlling external circumstances, but by mastering the art of companionship with your inner self.

Understanding the Self: Beyond Ego and Identity

To make this pact, we must first understand the self we are committing to. Often, our sense of self is entangled with the ego—a construct of stories, roles, and labels shaped by culture, childhood, and experience. This ego-self can be fickle, judgmental, and prone to self-criticism.

Yet beneath this surface lies a deeper essence—our true self, the indivisible unity of body and soul. This self is not defined by external validation or fleeting emotions but by an innate presence that witnesses all experiences with compassion and equanimity.

The pact *I am with me* is a vow to honour this true self. It is a promise to listen without judgment, to nurture without conditions, and to embrace both light and shadow within.

The Fear and Resistance to Commitment

Making such a pact may trigger resistance or fear. Why? Because it requires vulnerability—acknowledging our loneliness, imperfections, and past wounds. It challenges the habitual ways we have avoided ourselves through distraction, busyness, or self-denial.

Fear whispers: *What if I fail? What if I disappoint myself? What if I am not enough?*

These doubts are natural and must be met with gentleness. The pact is not about perfection but presence. It is not about relentless self-improvement but radical self-acceptance.

By embracing this vulnerability, we step into a new kind of strength—the courage to be fully ourselves, even in our brokenness.

The Elements of the Pact

This first pact can be understood through several interwoven commitments:

1. **To Listen Deeply:** I will listen to my body's sensations, my soul's whispers, and my mind's chatter without judgment or haste. I

will give myself the time and space to be heard.

2. **To Show Compassion:** I will treat myself with the same kindness and understanding I offer to my closest friends. I will honour my feelings and needs, even when they seem inconvenient.

3. **To Be Present:** I will show up for myself in every moment, whether joyful or painful. I will not abandon myself when discomfort arises but will hold myself gently through it.

4. **To Protect Boundaries:** I will respect my limits and say no to what drains me or harms me. I will create sacred space for rest, reflection, and renewal.

5. **To Celebrate Small Victories:** I will recognize and honour the efforts I make, no matter how small. Each step toward self-friendship is a triumph worth acknowledging.

6. **To Commit to Growth:** I will embrace the journey of self-discovery with curiosity and openness. I understand that being with myself is an evolving dance, not a fixed destination.

Ritualizing the Pact: Making It Tangible

Words are powerful, but the pact becomes real when we embody it through intentional practice. Creating a ritual around this commitment anchors it in your lived experience.

Here is one way to ritualize the pact:

- Find a quiet place where you can sit comfortably, free from distractions.
- Close your eyes and take several deep, grounding breaths.
- Reflect on the intention: "I choose to be with myself, to honour and cherish my presence."
- Speak the pact aloud or silently, using words that resonate with your heart. For example:

"I am with me. I am my own best friend, my loyal companion. I will listen, nurture, and protect myself through all of life's seasons."

- Place your hand over your heart or on your belly to feel the warmth and connection.
- Consider writing the pact down in a journal or creating a symbol—a drawing, a token, or a mantra—that you can revisit as a reminder.

This ritual is an act of self-Honouring and an invitation to deepen your inner relationship daily.

Living the Pact: Practical Applications

Making the pact is only the beginning. Living it requires ongoing commitment and gentle discipline. Here are some practical ways to honour *I am with me*:

- **Daily Check-ins:** Set aside moments each day to pause and ask yourself, "How am I feeling? What do I need right now?" Listen without judgment and respond with care.
- **Self-Care as Sacred Practice:** Approach self-care not as indulgence but as essential nourishment. Whether it's rest, nutritious food, movement, or creative expression, these are gifts you give to the sacred friendship with yourself.
- **Saying No with Love:** Recognize when your energy is stretched too thin. Saying no to others can be an act of saying yes to yourself.
- **Mindful Presence:** Engage fully in whatever you do, allowing yourself to be fully present with your experience rather than distracted or disconnected.
- **Embracing Imperfection:** When you stumble or fall into old patterns of neglect, remember that this is part of the human journey. Return to the pact with kindness and without shame.

The Ripple Effect: Healing Through Self-Companionship

Committing to be with yourself transforms not only your inner world but also your outer relationships. As your self-trust grows, you become less dependent on external approval and less reactive to others' judgments.

This newfound stability fosters healthier boundaries, deeper empathy, and more authentic connections. Paradoxically, by becoming your own best friend, you become a better friend to the world.

Philosophically, this pact echoes the wisdom of ancient teachings: self-love is the foundation from which all love flows. The body and soul, once estranged by neglect, become allies in the journey toward wholeness.

The Eternal Companion

In the vastness of existence, external friendships and circumstances may come and go. Yet the companionship between your body and soul endures beyond time, space, and change.

The first pact, *I am with me*, is a promise that transcends conditions. It is a sacred alliance to remain steadfast, to hold space for your own unfolding story, and to walk through life with the unwavering presence of your own best friend.

Practice for the Chapter:

Today, take a moment to make your own pact. Find a quiet space, breathe deeply, and speak or write your commitment to yourself. Return to this pact whenever you feel disconnected or uncertain. Let it be a beacon guiding you back to the enduring friendship within.

ELEVEN

SEEING THE BODY AS SACRED

Building Respect, Trust, and Gratitude for Your Body

In a world that often reduces the body to a mere object—a machine to be fixed, an aesthetic to be sculpted, or a vessel to be used—the profound truth of the body's sacredness is frequently lost. This chapter invites a radical shift in perception: to see the body not as an object or a burden, but as a holy temple, a sacred vessel that carries the essence of life, experience, and emotion. To honour the body in this way is to step into a deeper communion with ourselves, embracing the fullness of existence as it manifests through our physical form.

The Body as the Ground of Being

Philosophers, mystics, and sages throughout history have recognized that the body is not separate from the self but is the very ground in which selfhood arises. It is through the body that we perceive, feel, and engage with the world. Our breath, our heartbeat, our sensations—all these are the language through which life expresses itself.

To see the body as sacred is to recognize that it is the living presence of being in the physical realm. It is the meeting place where the intangible soul touches the tangible world. This body, with its imperfections and wonders, is the only home we have in this lifetime. To disregard or disdain it is to estrange ourselves from the very essence of existence.

From Objectification to Reverence

Modern society often teaches us to view the body through a narrow lens—its utility, appearance, or performance value. This objectification leads to fragmentation, where the body is treated as separate from the mind and soul, a possession to be controlled or modified according to external ideals.

This fragmented view alienates us from our bodies, fostering dissatisfaction, shame, and neglect. The sacred perspective, however, calls us to reverence—to treat the body as a living miracle, a sacred vessel worthy of respect and care.

Reverence is an attitude of profound honour and gratitude. It asks us to shift from judgment to acceptance, from exploitation to nurturing. The body becomes not a project but a partner, an ally in the journey of life.

The Body as a Storyteller

Every scar, every wrinkle, every ache, and every sensation tells a story. The body records our history in ways the mind cannot always articulate. It remembers trauma, joy, love, and loss. It holds memories of battles fought and victories won.

To see the body as sacred is to listen deeply to its stories without resistance or denial. Pain, for example, is not merely a problem to be eliminated but a messenger with wisdom to convey. Fatigue signals the need for rest; tension reveals emotional blocks; trembling can be a release of stored fears.

When we honour the body's storytelling, we invite healing to unfold organically, aligning our physical state with the deeper truths of our being.

Embodied Emotion: The Body as Emotional Archive

Emotions are not just mental phenomena but are deeply rooted in the body. When we feel anxiety, joy, grief, or love, these states manifest physically—through breath patterns, muscle tone, heart rate, and more.

The sacred body is an emotional archive, holding the imprint of every experience. By tuning into bodily sensations, we access an authentic emotional landscape, unfiltered by mental distortion or denial.

Philosophically, this insight aligns with the ancient wisdom that body and soul are inseparable. The soul's emotions resonate through the body's tissues, and healing arises when we acknowledge this intimate connection.

The Body as a Portal to Presence

To see the body as sacred is to recognize it as a portal to the present moment. The body exists only now; it cannot live in the past or the future. It invites us to inhabit the here and now fully.

Mindfulness practices emphasize this truth: by grounding awareness in bodily sensations—breath, touch, movement—we cultivate presence. Presence itself is sacred because it is the space where life unfolds unmediated.

The body is thus not just a container but a gateway, a threshold to deeper awareness and spiritual connection.

The Body in Ritual and Tradition

Across cultures and spiritual traditions, the body has been honoured as sacred through rituals, ceremonies, and practices. From sacred dances to anointing with oils, from fasting to yoga, these acts recognize the body as a holy instrument of the divine.

These rituals remind us that Honouring the body is not a superficial act but a profound spiritual practice. They teach us that the body deserves space for reverence, celebration, and healing.

Integrating such sacred practices into daily life can rekindle a sense of awe and gratitude for our embodied existence.

The Ethical Dimension: Caring for the Sacred Vessel

Seeing the body as sacred carries an ethical imperative: to care for it with reverence. This care is not limited to hygiene or nutrition but extends to how we speak to ourselves, how we move, how we rest, and how we protect our physical wellbeing.

Self-care becomes an act of sacred devotion, a way to honour the divine spark within. It means listening to the body's needs and responding with kindness rather than force or neglect.

In a world that glorifies productivity and often dismisses rest, this ethical stance is revolutionary. It invites a balance where activity and rest, effort and surrender, are harmonized in service of the whole self.

Embracing Impermanence and Change

The body is also a mirror of impermanence. It ages, changes, and eventually returns to the earth. To see it as sacred is not to deny this truth but to embrace it fully.

Impermanence teaches us to cherish the body in every moment, to honour its cycles, and to accept change as part of the sacred rhythm of life.

This acceptance fosters peace, releasing us from the tyranny of youth and appearance and inviting us to find beauty in every phase of embodiment.

The Body as a Source of Creativity and Wisdom

The body is not merely a vessel but a source of creative energy and wisdom. It moves, dances, expresses, and communicates in ways words cannot capture.

Artists, dancers, healers, and sages throughout time have attuned to the body's creative pulse, drawing from its deep well of inspiration.

Recognizing the body as a sacred creative force invites us to explore movement, touch, breath, and sensation as pathways to insight and transformation.

Practical Pathways to Sacred Embodiment

How do we begin to see and live with the body as sacred? Here are practical approaches to deepen this relationship:

- **Gratitude Practice:** Regularly express gratitude for your body's capabilities and resilience. Acknowledge the miraculous work it performs every moment.
- **Mindful Movement:** Engage in practices such as yoga, tai chi, or simple stretching that connect breath, body, and mind with intention and respect.

- **Body Awareness Meditation:** Spend time in quiet reflection tuning into bodily sensations without judgment, allowing the body's wisdom to emerge.
- **Nourishment:** Choose foods and drinks that honour your body's needs, fuelling it with respect and care.
- **Rest and Sleep:** Prioritize restorative rest as a sacred necessity, not a luxury.
- **Sacred Touch:** Whether through self-massage, gentle skin brushing, or therapeutic touch, honour the body through compassionate contact.
- **Creative Expression:** Explore dance, art, or movement as ways to celebrate and communicate through your body.

The Body-Soul Partnership

Ultimately, seeing the body as sacred is inseparable from Honouring the soul it carries. The body and soul are not two but one, intertwined in a sacred dance.

When we recognize this partnership, we begin to live in harmony—respecting our physical needs while nurturing our spiritual essence.

This holistic vision frees us from dualistic thinking and invites a fuller experience of what it means to be alive.

Conclusion: A Call to Reverence

This chapter is a call to awaken to the sacredness that has always been present in your body. To shift perception from object to temple, from machine to miracle.

As you begin to see your body as a sacred vessel, your relationship with yourself deepens and transforms. You step into a space of reverence, gratitude, and compassionate care.

This sacred view becomes a foundation for healing, presence, and wholeness—a vital step on the journey of self-friendship and soulful living.

Reflection Exercise:

Take a few moments today to honour your body in a tangible way. Perhaps place your hands gently on your heart or belly and silently acknowledge the sacred presence within. Reflect on what it means for you to see your body as more than an object—how might this shift change the way you live and love yourself?

TWELVE
Touch, Breath, and Movement

Three fundamental expressions—touch, breath, and movement—act as powerful portals through which we can rediscover and honour our bodies. In life's intricate rhythm, these simple yet profound practices ground us, offering a path to deeper awareness, healing, and connection with ourselves, reminding us to listen, feel, and move with intention and presence each day. These elemental forces are not mere mechanical functions or casual experiences; they are sacred rituals through which we awaken to our embodied presence. This chapter invites a deep exploration into how the conscious engagement with touch, breath, and movement can restore the intimate relationship between body and soul, fostering healing, awareness, and holistic well-being.

The Primacy of Touch: The Language of Connection

Touch is the earliest language we ever know. Long before words or concepts arise, our first experience of existence is felt through contact—skin to skin, warmth to warmth. From the comforting embrace of a mother to the gentle brush of a leaf in the wind, touch grounds us in reality and in connection.

Philosophically, touch is the language through which the body communicates both with the external world and the inner self. It is through touch that we feel safe, seen, and acknowledged. This primal form of communication bridges the invisible gap between self and other, inner and outer, self and soul.

When we consciously engage in touch—whether self-touch, massage, or holding hands with another—we awaken a sacred dialogue. The skin, our largest sensory organ, becomes a portal to healing. It releases tension, soothes pain, and transmits care and love.

The absence or numbness of touch often leads to disconnection and loneliness. In modern life, many suffer from "touch starvation," a deprivation of healthy physical contact, which disrupts emotional and physical health. Reclaiming touch as a ritual is thus a vital step towards Honouring our embodied selves.

The Sacred Art of Self-Touch

Touching oneself with kindness and awareness is a practice of sacred reverence. It transforms touch from a purely functional act into an expression of love and acceptance. Whether it's the gentle stroke of the face, the placing of hands over the heart, or a tender embrace of one's own limbs, self-touch anchors us to the present moment and the reality of our embodied being.

This sacred self-contact offers a profound antidote to self-criticism and alienation. It is a way of saying, "I see you. I honour you. You are worthy." When the hands become instruments of compassion toward the body, healing is invited at both physical and emotional levels.

Breath: The Bridge Between Body and Soul

Breath is the silent thread weaving together body and soul. It is the vital force that animates life, the rhythm that connects us to the universe. Unlike most bodily functions, breath is both involuntary and voluntary—a unique bridge between the conscious and unconscious realms.

Philosophically, breath is often understood as prana, qi, or life energy. It is the pulse of existence, the sacred rhythm that carries the soul within the vessel of the body.

When we breathe deeply and consciously, we activate a profound presence. The breath becomes an anchor, a tool for grounding awareness in the now. It carries us beyond mental chatter and into the spaciousness of being.

Breath is also a tool of transformation. Through intentional breathing practices, we can influence our emotional states, calm the nervous system, and release stored tensions within the body.

The Power of Conscious Breathing

In everyday life, our breath is often shallow, fragmented, or hurried, reflecting and reinforcing stress, anxiety, or disconnection. To cultivate conscious breathing is to reclaim the body's natural state of ease and vitality.

Techniques such as diaphragmatic breathing, alternate nostril breathing, or extended exhalation engage the parasympathetic nervous system, inviting relaxation and balance. Breath becomes a meditation, a prayer, a sacred ritual performed thousands of times a day without awareness—until we invite mindfulness into it.

Philosophically, breathing is a symbol of the eternal dance between presence and flow, inhalation and exhalation, coming and going. By Honouring the breath, we honour the very essence of life itself.

Movement: The Body's Expression of Being

Movement is the dynamic expression of life coursing through the body. It is the language of freedom, creativity, and vitality. To move consciously is to listen deeply to the body's wisdom and to allow the soul to express itself through form.

In many ancient traditions, movement is not merely physical exercise but a sacred ritual. Whether through yoga, dance, martial arts, or simple mindful walking, movement is a dialogue between the inner world and outer expression.

Philosophically, movement embodies the principle of impermanence and flow. It reflects the constant change and renewal that characterize existence. When we move with awareness, we align ourselves with the natural rhythms of life.

Movement as Meditation and Healing

When practiced with presence, movement becomes a form of meditation—an active mindfulness that unites body, mind, and soul. Every gesture, step, or stretch is an opportunity to reconnect with ourselves.

This mindful movement allows us to release tension, awaken energy centres, and restore balance. It is a healing art that supports emotional expression, physical health, and spiritual awakening.

The body remembers trauma and joy alike through its patterns of movement. Relearning to move with freedom and grace is a reclaiming of self, a healing of past wounds, and a celebration of life's flow.

Integrating Touch, Breath, and Movement: The Triad of Embodied Ritual

While each—touch, breath, and movement—holds its own sacred power, their integration forms a holistic practice of embodied presence. Together, they create a triad that grounds us in the body, awakens the soul, and opens a pathway to healing and wholeness.

- **Touch** invites us into the tactile reality of being.
- **Breath** carries us into the invisible flow of life energy.
- **Movement** expresses the dynamic unfolding of existence.

When practiced together, these rituals cultivate a profound self-friendship. They help dissolve the barriers of numbness and distraction, bringing us back to our true home—the living body.

Practical Pathways to Ritual

To cultivate these practices in daily life, consider these simple yet powerful rituals:

- **Morning Breath Awareness:** Before rising, take a few moments to observe your breath. Breathe deeply and slowly, inviting calm and presence.
- **Self-Touch Check-in:** Place your hands gently on your heart or belly throughout the day. Feel the warmth, pressure, and connection.

- **Mindful Movement Breaks:** Incorporate moments of conscious stretching, walking, or dancing. Notice how your body responds, what sensations arise.
- **Evening Gratitude Touch:** Before sleep, caress your face or arms with kindness, acknowledging the body's efforts through the day.
- **Breath-Movement Meditation:** Combine breath awareness with slow, flowing movement—such as yoga or tai chi—as a ritual to embody presence fully.

Overcoming Barriers: Resistance and Disconnection

Many people experience resistance or discomfort when engaging with these embodied rituals. This can stem from past trauma, cultural conditioning, or self-judgment.

It is important to approach these practices with gentleness and patience. Honour where you are. Begin slowly. Use these moments not as tasks but as invitations to intimacy with yourself.

The body remembers what the mind often forgets: that we are whole, worthy, and deeply connected to life.

The Philosophical Invitation: Embodiment as Liberation

To embrace touch, breath, and movement is to answer a profound philosophical call: the call to embodiment. Embodiment is liberation from the tyranny of disembodied thought and fragmentation.

It is a reclaiming of the body as a sacred home, a temple of the soul, and a dynamic field of awareness.

This liberation is not about perfection or control but about presence, acceptance, and reverence.

Conclusion: Returning Home to Yourself

As you engage with the sacred rituals of touch, breath, and movement, you return home to your body and soul. You awaken a friendship that has always been waiting—patient, loving, and true.

This chapter invites you to honour these gifts daily, to cultivate rituals that reconnect you to your embodied essence, and to move forward with a renewed sense of wholeness.

Reflection Exercise:

Set aside ten minutes today to practice a simple ritual combining touch, breath, and movement. Place your hands gently on your chest. Breathe deeply three times. Then, gently stretch your arms overhead or sway your body side to side. Notice how your body responds. Allow yourself to receive this time as an act of sacred self-friendship.

THIRTEEN

FOOD AS COMMUNICATION

In the vast ocean of our connection with the body, food holds a deeply personal and multifaceted place. It is not merely fuel or a means of sustenance, but a form of communication—a continuous exchange between our inner self and the physical form that supports us. Through food, we express care, emotion, memory, and the way we nurture the body that carries us through life. How we approach eating, the awareness we bring to it, and the messages we receive in return can deeply influence our connection to our body and soul.

This chapter invites a philosophical journey into the sacred art of mindful eating, uncovering how food acts as a language through which the body speaks, reveals needs, and fosters trust. Through learning to listen attentively to hunger, fullness, and pleasure, we begin to cultivate a nourishing relationship that transcends mere nutrition and embraces the wholeness of being.

The Language of Food: Beyond Fuel

At first glance, eating may appear as a straightforward biological necessity—an act to satisfy hunger and provide energy. Yet, when approached without awareness, it often becomes a mechanical process, disconnected from the deeper needs and wisdom of the body.

Philosophically, food is a form of sacred communication. It is an offering from the earth, a gift from nature, that nourishes not only the body but also the spirit. Every bite is an interaction with the world around us and with ourselves. Eating mindfully is thus an opportunity to engage in a sacred conversation—an exchange of respect, awareness, and care.

Food carries not only chemical nutrients but also energetic qualities, cultural meanings, and emotional resonance. It embodies a language that speaks to the body's cravings, memories, and longings. When we listen carefully, food reveals messages about balance, deficiency, pleasure, and healing.

The Body's Wisdom: Hunger and Fullness as Guides

Two fundamental signals form the cornerstone of this communication: hunger and fullness. They are the body's way of inviting us to respond with care and presence.

Hunger is the body's call for nourishment, a primal urge that signals a genuine need. But hunger is not only physical; it is intertwined with emotional and energetic layers. True hunger feels grounded, steady, and patient—a respectful request rather than an urgent demand.

On the other hand, **fullness** signals that the body's needs have been met. Recognizing fullness requires a subtle awareness, a willingness to pause and listen. It is an invitation to stop, rest, and integrate.

In modern culture, these signals are often ignored, overridden, or confused. We eat for reasons beyond sustenance—stress, boredom, celebration, distraction—which clouds the clarity of communication.

By cultivating mindful eating, we reclaim the body's wisdom. We learn to differentiate between true hunger and emotional cravings, between nourishing fullness and overindulgence. This discernment becomes a foundation of trust—a promise that the body will be listened to, honoured, and cared for.

Pleasure: The Soul's Invitation in Eating

Eating is not merely functional; it is also an experience of pleasure. The taste, texture, aroma, and colour of food evoke joy and satisfaction that ripple through body and soul. This pleasure is not indulgence or excess but a sacred expression of delight—a celebration of life's abundance.

Philosophically, pleasure in eating connects us to the soul's longing for beauty, harmony, and enjoyment. It is a form of gratitude for the gifts we receive and an affirmation of our right to joy.

Mindful eating honours this dimension of pleasure by inviting us to savour each bite fully, to engage all senses, and to be present with the moment. Pleasure becomes a form of communication—an acknowledgment of the body's delight and a nurturing of the soul's happiness.

When pleasure is embraced without guilt or shame, it fosters balance and well-being. It becomes a bridge that unites nourishment with joy, body with soul.

Mindful Eating: A Practice of Presence and Respect

Mindful eating is the conscious act of bringing full attention and respect to the experience of eating. It involves slowing down, observing sensations, and tuning into the body's signals.

Key aspects of mindful eating include:

- **Awareness of Sensations:** Noticing the textures, flavours, smells, and temperatures of food.
- **Listening to Hunger and Fullness:** Checking in before, during, and after eating.
- **Gratitude:** Acknowledging the journey of food—from earth to table, from nature to body.
- **Non-Judgment:** Letting go of critical thoughts about what, how much, or how fast we eat.
- **Presence:** Being fully in the moment, avoiding distractions such as screens or multitasking.

Through these practices, eating becomes a sacred ritual—a moment of communion with the self and the natural world.

Breaking Free from Conditioned Patterns

Many of us come to eating with layers of conditioning—cultural beliefs, family habits, emotional associations, and societal messages about body image and diet. These layers often obscure the natural dialogue with the body.

For example, we may eat to cope with stress, to reward ourselves, or to numb uncomfortable feelings. We may also judge ourselves harshly for eating certain foods or amounts, leading to cycles of restriction and bingeing.

This chapter encourages readers to explore these patterns compassionately, recognizing them as survival strategies rather than failures. By gently peeling back these layers, we create space for authentic listening and trust.

Mindful eating becomes a tool to dismantle these conditioned responses and to build a new relationship grounded in respect, kindness, and presence.

Food as Medicine and Ceremony

Throughout history, food has been recognized not only for its physical benefits but also as medicine and sacred ceremony. Many cultures honour food with rituals that acknowledge its life-giving power and its role in healing.

Philosophically, food connects us to the cycles of nature, the changing seasons, and the community that nurtures us. Eating mindfully is thus an act of reverence—acknowledging the interconnectedness of all life.

By approaching food as medicine and ceremony, we deepen our appreciation and awareness. This perspective transforms everyday meals into opportunities for healing, gratitude, and spiritual connection.

Listening to Cravings: Messages from the Body and Soul

Cravings often carry important messages. They may signal nutrient deficiencies, emotional needs, or subconscious desires. Rather than suppress or shame cravings, mindful eating invites us to approach them with curiosity and respect.

For example, a sudden craving for sweet foods might indicate a need for comfort or emotional soothing, while a craving for crunchy vegetables may signal a need for grounding or stimulation.

By listening attentively to cravings, we learn to differentiate between bodily needs and emotional urges. This discernment enhances self-trust and empowers conscious choices.

Cultivating Trust: The Foundation of Food Communication

At the heart of mindful eating is trust—a deep, unwavering trust in the body's intelligence and its ability to guide us toward what it truly needs.

Trust is built gradually through attentive listening, compassionate response, and consistent practice. As we honour hunger, fullness, and pleasure, we create a safe and respectful dialogue with our body.

This trust extends beyond food choices; it nurtures a broader sense of safety, belonging, and self-love. It becomes a foundation upon which the friendship between body and soul can flourish.

Practical Steps to Cultivate Mindful Eating

To begin or deepen the practice of mindful eating, consider the following:

- **Pause Before Eating:** Take a moment to check in with your hunger level. Are you eating because you are truly hungry or for another reason?
- **Engage the Senses:** Notice the colours, textures, and aromas of your food before taking a bite.
- **Chew Slowly:** Savor each bite, allowing time for taste to fully register.
- **Put Down Utensils:** Between bites, set down your fork or spoon to bring awareness back to the act of eating.
- **Notice Fullness:** Pay attention to signs of satisfaction and stop eating before feeling overly full.
- **Express Gratitude:** Thank the food, the earth, and your body for the nourishment received.

The Philosophical Invitation: Food as Dialogue with Self

Mindful eating invites us into a deeper philosophical understanding of food—not merely as sustenance, but as an ongoing dialogue with our body and soul.

Each meal becomes a moment of presence, respect, and connection. The act of eating transforms into a sacred exchange, where the body's needs are heard, the soul's pleasure honoured, and the whole self embraced.

In this dialogue, food is both teacher and healer, a bridge between the physical and the spiritual, a manifestation of life's profound interconnectedness.

Conclusion: Building a Lifelong Friendship with Food and Self

As you cultivate mindful eating, you begin to restore a trusting, loving relationship with your body. Food becomes a friend, a messenger, and a ritual of care.

This chapter encourages embracing food as communication, listening with curiosity and kindness, and honouring the body's wisdom in every meal.

By doing so, you nurture the vital friendship between body and soul—one that will sustain you not only till the end but beyond.

Reflection Exercise:

Today, try a mindful eating practice with one meal or snack. Before eating, pause and ask: "Am I hungry? What does my body truly need right now?" As you eat, engage your senses fully. Afterward, reflect on how your body feels and what messages it may be sending.

FOURTEEN

LISTENING INSTEAD OF OVERRIDING

In the relentless pace of modern life, a pervasive attitude often governs our relationship with our bodies and souls: the impulse to override, to push through, to ignore discomfort and exhaustion in the name of productivity, duty, or survival. This

habitual suppression of inner signals is not only unsustainable but fundamentally alienates us from our deepest selves. Chapter 14 invites a profound philosophical exploration of the art and practice of *listening*—an intentional choice to honour the body and soul's language rather than silencing it.

We will uncover the cost of overriding, the liberating power of respect for internal signals, and the path toward a more compassionate, attentive way of being with ourselves.

The Culture of Overriding: An Existential Dilemma

From early on, many of us learn a narrative of strength as endurance—the ability to keep going despite pain, fatigue, or discomfort. Cultural values often equate worth with productivity, and vulnerability with weakness. This social conditioning encourages overriding the body's whispers in favour of external demands.

Philosophically, this reveals a tragic paradox: to live fully, we must listen deeply; yet society often prizes the opposite—silencing, control, and relentless doing. This paradox fuels an existential dilemma. We are torn between Honouring our inner experience and meeting the relentless expectations of the outer world.

In this chapter, we confront this dilemma, recognizing that the impulse to override is a survival mechanism—a way to navigate an often overwhelming reality—but also a disconnection from our essence.

The Cost of Overriding: Fragmentation and Exhaustion

When we override, we fracture our relationship with ourselves. The body and soul, craving acknowledgment, resort to louder signals—pain, illness, anxiety—to demand attention.

This fragmentation manifests physically as chronic fatigue, pain, and illness; emotionally as irritability, numbness, and anxiety; and spiritually as emptiness, confusion, and despair.

Overriding erodes the very foundation of self-trust. When we ignore our internal wisdom, we send the message that our needs are secondary or unworthy. Over time, this breeds a disowned self, hidden beneath layers of denial and distraction.

Philosophically, the body and soul can be seen as a unified field of communication. Ignoring one aspect disrupts the whole. Thus, overriding leads not to strength but fragility.

Listening as a Radical Act of Respect

To listen instead of overriding is a radical act of respect—respect for the self as a living, sentient being deserving of care.

Listening requires slowing down, turning inward, and surrendering control. It demands courage, for to truly hear our discomfort or exhaustion is to acknowledge vulnerability.

Yet, listening opens the door to healing. It fosters a dialogue that nurtures integration rather than fragmentation. Respectful listening restores self-trust and invites the body and soul back into companionship.

This act of listening is revolutionary in a culture that prizes relentless doing. It becomes a declaration of sovereignty—a reclaiming of the right to be seen, heard, and honoured.

The Philosophy of Attention: Presence as Medicine

Philosophers and mystics throughout history have emphasized the transformative power of attention. To *pay attention* is not merely to observe but to engage with full presence and intention.

Attention is the medicine that heals the split between self and experience. When we attend to exhaustion or discomfort without judgment, we transform these signals from obstacles into guides.

This chapter explores how attention functions as a bridge between inner experience and conscious choice, inviting readers to cultivate presence as a foundational skill.

Recognizing the Body's Boundaries: Permission to Pause

One of the most profound lessons in listening is learning to recognize and respect the body's boundaries. These boundaries are sacred limits—thresholds that when crossed, lead to harm.

Yet, many of us grow up with the implicit belief that boundaries are weaknesses to be overcome. We push through tiredness, pain, or emotional overwhelm as if these signs were enemies.

Instead, we are invited to see boundaries as gifts—protective signals that call us to pause, reflect, and restore.

Permission to pause is an act of self-compassion and wisdom. It acknowledges that rest and recovery are essential elements of vitality, not signs of failure.

The Language of Discomfort: Understanding Messages Beneath the Surface

Discomfort is often perceived as something to be fixed or eradicated. But discomfort—be it physical, emotional, or spiritual—is a messenger carrying valuable information.

This chapter encourages readers to shift perspective and develop curiosity toward discomfort. What story does this fatigue tell? What unmet need or unresolved tension lies beneath this pain?

By developing this skill of inquiry, we move from resistance to receptivity. Discomfort ceases to be a foe and becomes a teacher, guiding us back to wholeness.

Tools for Listening: Practices to Cultivate Inner Awareness

Listening deeply requires practice. The chapter offers practical tools that cultivate inner awareness and build the habit of respectful attention:

- **Body Scanning:** A gentle practice of moving awareness systematically through the body, noticing sensations without judgment.
- **Journaling:** Writing reflections on moments of discomfort or exhaustion to uncover patterns and insights.
- **Breath Awareness:** Using the breath as an anchor to remain present with internal states.
- **Pause Rituals:** Creating small moments of stillness throughout the day to check in with the body and soul.
- **Asking Gentle Questions:** Posing non-judgmental inquiries like "What do I need right now?" or "What is this feeling trying to tell me?"

Through consistent practice, these tools deepen the capacity to listen and respond with kindness.

Overcoming Resistance: The Challenge of Surrender

Despite the benefits, listening instead of overriding is often met with internal resistance. The mind may fear loss of control, productivity, or identity. The ego, accustomed to dominance, balks at surrender.

This chapter philosophically explores this resistance as part of the human condition. Resistance is not a flaw but an invitation to deeper trust and humility.

Surrender here is not defeat but a conscious yielding—a brave choice to honour limits and embrace vulnerability.

This nuanced understanding reframes surrender as an empowered, sacred act.

Listening in Relationships: Extending Respect Beyond the Self

While the primary focus is internal listening, the chapter also reflects on how this practice enriches relationships. When we learn to listen to ourselves with respect, we naturally extend that listening to others.

Philosophically, authentic relationships are built on mutual presence and attentiveness. By cultivating listening within, we cultivate empathy, patience, and connection without.

This ripple effect amplifies the power of listening as a force for healing in both personal and collective spheres.

The Path Forward: Making Listening a Lifestyle

To listen instead of overriding is not a one-time act but a lifelong commitment. It requires ongoing vigilance, patience, and self-compassion.

This chapter closes with an invitation to integrate listening into daily life, transforming it from occasional practice to a guiding principle.

Readers are encouraged to view listening as a sacred pact with themselves—a promise to honour their body and soul with respect and kindness through all seasons of life.

Reflection Exercise:

Set aside five minutes each day for a "listening pause." Close your eyes, breathe deeply, and ask: "What is my body trying to tell me right now? What is my soul yearning for?" Record any insights without judgment. Over time, notice how your relationship with exhaustion, discomfort, and limits transforms.

FIFTEEN

BODY IMAGE VS. BODY TRUTH

In a world saturated by images—photoshopped, filtered, curated—our perception of the body is often distorted. The "body image" we carry is shaped by cultural ideals, media narratives, and social expectations that define beauty narrowly and often unrealistically. These images, though pervasive, represent not the living, breathing reality of our bodies but an illusion—a constructed ideal that can distance us from our authentic bodily experience.

Chapter 15 invites a philosophical journey to disentangle body image from body truth. It encourages a return to a foundational way of knowing: how the body *feels*, not how it *looks*. Through this exploration, readers learn to honour the body as it truly is—a vessel of experience, sensation, and life—beyond external appearances.

The Mirage of Beauty: How Culture Shapes Body Image

To understand the conflict between body image and body truth, we must first recognize the forces shaping body image. Cultural norms project ideals of beauty—slimness, youth, flawless skin—that often exclude the rich diversity of human bodies.

Philosophically, these ideals are abstractions, symbolic forms created and maintained by collective agreement. They do not stem from lived experience but from ideals imposed externally.

The relentless exposure to such images conditions the mind to judge worth based on appearance. This breeds dissatisfaction and alienation from the body itself.

The body becomes an object to be perfected or controlled, rather than a living subject to be embraced and respected.

The Illusion of Separation: Body as Object vs. Body as Subject

At the heart of this chapter lies a profound philosophical distinction: viewing the body as an *object* versus experiencing it as a *subject*.

When we focus on body image, we objectify our bodies—reducing them to forms to be seen, judged, or compared. This objectification alienates us from our embodied subjectivity, the rich inner world of sensations, movements, and feelings.

Body truth, in contrast, emerges from the lived experience of the body as a subject. It is accessed through attention to sensation, rhythm, breath, and the subtle communication the body offers.

Reclaiming this subjectivity invites a more intimate, compassionate relationship with the body.

The Philosophy of Embodiment: Being Present in the Flesh

Embodiment is the philosophical notion that consciousness is not separate from the body but inseparable—a unified lived experience.

To embody is to live fully in the present moment, rooted in sensory awareness and physical presence.

This contrasts with the dissociation that often accompanies preoccupation with body image, where the body is seen as a thing to be manipulated or judged rather than a site of experience.

Embodiment teaches us to trust the body's wisdom, to listen to its needs, and to honour its rhythms.

Feeling Over Seeing: Returning to Sensation

One of the chapter's central invitations is to prioritize *feeling* over *seeing*.

Seeing, especially in the cultural sense, is laden with judgment, comparison, and ideals. It often reinforces the divide between self and body.

Feeling, by contrast, is direct, immediate, and nonjudgmental. It invites curiosity and presence.

By cultivating attention to bodily sensations—warmth, tension, breath, ease—readers reconnect with the body's truth beyond visual form.

This sensory awareness opens pathways to self-acceptance and healing.

The Body's Language of Comfort and Discomfort

The body speaks through sensations of comfort and discomfort. Comfort signals alignment and balance; discomfort indicates imbalance or unmet needs.

Yet, when fixated on body image, discomfort is often experienced as a threat to self-worth. This reaction perpetuates cycles of denial, criticism, and self-rejection.

Instead, embracing discomfort as meaningful communication invites gentle inquiry: What is this sensation telling me? Where is my body calling for care or attention?

This shift from judgment to curiosity transforms the relationship with the body's messages.

Beyond Appearance: The Body as a Vessel of Experience

Our bodies carry more than skin and bones—they are vessels of memories, emotions, and life stories.

Philosophically, the body is a living archive, inscribed with joy, pain, resilience, and transformation.

This deeper understanding encourages readers to see their bodies not merely as physical forms but as sacred repositories of their unique existence.

Honouring this fullness nurtures a profound gratitude and respect that transcends superficial appearance.

The Practice of Loving Presence: Exercises to Connect with Body Truth

To cultivate connection with body truth, the chapter offers practical, experiential exercises:

- **Sensory Awareness Practice:** Sitting quietly, focusing on breath and noticing physical sensations without judgment. Simply observing warmth, coolness, pressure, or ease.
- **Body Gratitude Ritual:** Reflecting on the functions and gifts of the body—its ability to move, feel, heal, and sustain life.
- **Mirror Compassion Exercise:** Looking gently in the mirror, speaking kindly to oneself, acknowledging the body's reality without critique.
- **Movement Meditation:** Engaging in slow, mindful movement such as yoga or tai chi to deepen embodiment and reconnect with sensation.
- **Journal Reflection:** Writing about moments when the body felt alive, strong, or peaceful, emphasizing internal experience over external appearance.

Through these practices, readers nurture a grounded, embodied presence that honours body truth.

Navigating the Shadow: When Body Image Hurts

The chapter also addresses the painful shadow side of body image—the shame, self-criticism, and alienation many endure.

Philosophically, shame is a barrier to embodiment, a form of disconnection that silences the body's voice.

Healing shame requires gentle witnessing and compassionate presence. Recognizing that body image struggles are often symptoms of deeper wounds helps shift blame away from the self.

This awareness opens the door to self-forgiveness and renewed connection.

Embracing Impermanence: The Body's Changing Nature

Bodies are not static. They age, change, heal, and transform over time.

Resistance to this impermanence fuels body image anxiety and fear.

Philosophy teaches acceptance of impermanence as a natural law—a flow that includes growth, decay, and renewal.

By embracing change, readers learn to appreciate their bodies at every stage as expressions of life's unfolding mystery.

This acceptance deepens respect for body truth beyond superficial fixations.

The Collective Dimension: Challenging Societal Narratives

While the focus is deeply personal, the chapter acknowledges the collective dimension of body image.

Changing cultural narratives around beauty and worth is part of reclaiming body truth.

Readers are encouraged to critically examine media messages and social conditioning, cultivating awareness of how external narratives shape internal experience.

This awareness empowers choice—to embrace diverse, authentic body expressions rather than conform to limiting ideals.

The Path to Freedom: Embodying Acceptance and Compassion

The chapter closes with an invitation to embody freedom—a freedom born from acceptance and compassion.

By listening to how the body feels and honouring its truths, readers reclaim agency over their self-perception.

This freedom is a radical departure from the tyranny of body image. It restores a profound friendship with the body—a friendship grounded in truth, kindness, and presence.

Reflection Exercise:

Take a moment each day to notice one physical sensation—warmth, coolness, tension, or ease. Rather than judging, simply observe and welcome it. Reflect: How does my body *feel* right now? How does this sensation invite me to care for myself?

SIXTEEN

THE HEALING POWER OF SLEEP

Sleep—an inevitable, mysterious passage each night—holds profound power to heal and restore not only the body but the soul. In a world that prizes productivity and constant activity, sleep is often undervalued, seen as mere downtime or even a weakness. Yet, philosophically and practically, sleep is one of the deepest acts of self-care and restoration available to us. This chapter explores the intricate relationship between sleep, body, and soul, and how quality rest restores their vital connection, bringing clarity, renewal, and balance.

Sleep as a Sacred Pause

At its essence, sleep is a sacred pause—a deliberate surrender to stillness and unconsciousness that resets the living system. The body and soul, often fragmented by the demands of the waking world, find in sleep a space to harmonize and heal.

Philosophically, sleep invites us to embrace the rhythm of life that moves beyond constant doing into being. It is a reminder that life cycles between activity and rest, light and darkness, engagement and withdrawal.

This rhythm is fundamental to our wholeness. Without sleep, the body's processes falter, and the soul's voice becomes muffled.

The Body's Nighttime Repair

Biologically, sleep is when the body repairs tissues, consolidates memories, balances hormones, and rejuvenates the immune system. Wounds begin to heal; muscles relax; cells regenerate.

This biological repair reflects a deeper truth: the body's wisdom and capacity for self-healing are vast, but they require rest to function optimally.

Ignoring or shortening sleep interrupts this sacred repair cycle, leading to exhaustion, illness, and disconnection from bodily awareness.

The Soul's Nocturnal Journey

Beyond the physical, sleep invites the soul to journey inward and beyond. Dreams emerge as the language of the soul, weaving symbols, emotions, and insights.

Philosophers and mystics have long regarded dreams as a bridge to the unconscious and a form of soul communication. In sleep, the soul releases the day's burdens and processes subtle emotional and spiritual currents.

This nocturnal journey nurtures inner clarity and spiritual growth.

Sleep as Integration: Body and Soul in Harmony

Sleep serves as an integrative process, bringing together body and soul into renewed alignment.

Throughout the waking day, body and soul may become fragmented by stress, distraction, or conflict. Sleep reunites these aspects by allowing the mind to rest and the soul to engage in healing.

In this restful state, unconscious wisdom emerges, clarifying unresolved tensions and opening space for renewed vitality.

The Modern Sleep Crisis: Disconnection and Its Consequences

Modern life, with its artificial light, technology, and relentless pace, disrupts natural sleep rhythms. Many suffer from sleep deprivation, insomnia, or poor-quality rest.

Philosophically, this crisis represents a collective alienation from the body's needs and the soul's rhythms.

The consequences extend beyond fatigue: emotional instability, weakened intuition, impaired judgment, and spiritual disconnection.

Recognizing sleep's role as sacred restoration can help reverse this crisis.

Cultivating Sleep as Ritual

To harness sleep's healing power, cultivating intentional sleep rituals is essential. These rituals signal to body and soul that it is time to slow down and enter restorative rest.

Simple practices include:

- **Gentle winding down:** Dim lights, calm activities, avoiding screens.
- **Mindful breathing:** Slow, deep breaths to calm nervous systems.
- **Gratitude reflection:** A moment of appreciation to soothe the mind.
- **Comfortable environment:** A cool, dark, quiet space to invite sleep.

Rituals honour the body's natural rhythms and prepare the soul for the journey inward.

Philosophical Reflections on Sleep and Identity

Sleep also challenges our notions of identity. In sleep, consciousness shifts, self-awareness dims, and a liminal state emerges.

This invites reflection: Is the self-fixed and continuous, or fluid and changing? How does the experience of surrender in sleep reveal the nature of who we are?

Philosophy invites us to see sleep as a metaphor for letting go—of control, of ego, and of separation—leading to deeper connection with the whole self.

Sleep's Role in Emotional Healing

Sleep profoundly influences emotional processing. During sleep, the brain processes and integrates emotional experiences, reducing reactivity and enhancing resilience.

A lack of sleep amplifies stress, anxiety, and mood disturbances.

By Honouring sleep, we nurture emotional balance and compassion, essential for a harmonious relationship with ourselves.

The Intersection of Sleep and Intuition

Quality sleep sharpens intuition and inner knowing. Dreams, silence, and subconscious processing during sleep open channels to insight beyond rational thought.

Ignoring sleep dulls these intuitive capacities, leaving us disconnected from our soul's whispers.

Embracing sleep as sacred deepens trust in our inner wisdom.

Resistance to Sleep: Cultural and Psychological Barriers

Many resist sleep—whether due to work demands, anxiety, or fear of vulnerability. This resistance often reflects deeper issues: fear of silence, loss of control, or avoidance of inner truths.

Philosophically, this resistance is a form of self-alienation, a refusal to embrace the body-soul unity that sleep restores.

Recognizing and gently addressing this resistance opens the way for healing.

Practical Guidance for Deep Rest

- **Consistent sleep schedule:** Align with natural circadian rhythms.
- **Avoid stimulants:** Limit caffeine and heavy meals before bedtime.
- **Body relaxation techniques:** Progressive muscle relaxation, gentle yoga.
- **Mindful dream journaling:** Record dreams to engage the soul's messages.
- **Embracing naps:** Short rests can restore energy and clarity.

These habits cultivate a sanctuary for the body and soul to heal.

Embracing the Mystery of Sleep

Finally, sleep remains a mystery—where consciousness fades and the soul roams in realms unseen.

This mystery invites humility and wonder. It calls us to surrender and trust in life's deeper rhythms beyond our control.

Embracing this mystery nurtures peace and reverence for our embodied existence.

Closing Reflection

Sleep is not merely a physical necessity but a sacred encounter—a nightly invitation to reconnect with the depths of our being. Through quality rest, the body repairs, the soul communicates, and clarity arises. In Honouring sleep, we honour ourselves, embracing the profound companionship of body and soul that sustains us until the end and beyond.

SEVENTEEN
EMOTIONS LIVE IN THE FLESH

Emotions are often thought of as ethereal, intangible experiences—flights of the mind or fleeting feelings that pass like clouds in the sky. Yet, this view only tells part of the story. A profound truth lies deeper: emotions are embodied; they live, breathe, and manifest within the flesh. They are not simply housed in the mind or spirit but are intricately woven into the very fibres of our physical being. Understanding this intimate connection between emotion and body is crucial for holistic self-awareness and healing.

This chapter embarks on a philosophical exploration of how emotions are stored in the body, the ways in which they manifest physically, and how releasing this somatic tension can lead to liberation, balance, and unity between body and soul.

The Body as the Vessel of Emotion

The body is not merely a container for the mind and soul—it is an active participant in our emotional life. Every feeling we experience sends ripples through the body, shaping posture, muscle tone, breath, and even cellular memory.

Philosophers and healers throughout history—from Aristotle's view of the body-mind unity to contemporary somatic psychology—have recognized that body and emotion form an inseparable union. Emotions sculpt the body's landscape, and in turn, the body holds archives of past emotional experiences.

Consider the metaphor of the body as a living manuscript where emotions write their stories, sometimes visibly through tears or laughter, and sometimes invisibly through subtle muscular tensions or bodily sensations.

The Language of Tension and Sensation

Tension in the shoulders, tightness in the chest, knots in the stomach—these are not random or merely physical ailments. They are the body's language, speaking in a dialect of sensation and restriction, signalling unresolved emotional energy.

When joy wells up, the chest might open wide, breath flows freely, and muscles soften. Conversely, when grief, fear, or anger is suppressed, the body contracts—holding breath, tightening muscles, creating blocks that are felt as pain or discomfort.

These bodily manifestations serve as messages from the body to the conscious mind, reminders of emotions unexpressed or avoided.

The Historical Divide: Mind vs. Body

Western philosophy has long tended to separate mind from body, treating emotions as psychological phenomena and physical symptoms as purely biological. This dualism has led many to overlook the somatic dimension of emotion.

In recent decades, this divide has begun to dissolve as integrative health and somatic therapies highlight the body's role in emotional processing. Understanding emotions as embodied experiences challenges the mind-body split and calls us toward greater integration.

Emotions as Energy in Motion

The root of the word "emotion" — from Latin *emovere* meaning "to move out"—suggests that emotions are energies that must flow. When this flow is interrupted or blocked, the energy becomes trapped, creating physical stiffness, pain, or chronic tension.

Philosophically, emotions are not static states but dynamic processes that demand expression and release.

Recognizing emotions as energy invites us to listen to bodily signals as invitations to restore movement and flow, rather than obstacles to be ignored or forcibly controlled.

Where Emotions Commonly Reside in the Body

Different emotions tend to gather in characteristic bodily locations:

- **Anxiety and fear:** Often felt as tightness in the chest, shallow breathing, and tension in the shoulders or neck.
- **Anger:** Frequently held in clenched jaws, fists, or tight abdominal muscles.
- **Sadness and grief:** Felt as heaviness in the chest, lump in the throat, or tightness in the diaphragm.
- **Joy and love:** Associated with openness in the heart area, relaxed muscles, and lightness in the body.

These patterns are unique to individuals but share universal threads, reflecting the body's attempt to process emotional experience.

The Weight of Unexpressed Emotion

When emotions are denied or suppressed—whether due to cultural conditioning, trauma, or personal habits—they become lodged in the body as tension or pain. This stored emotional weight often manifests as chronic conditions such as migraines, digestive issues, or muscle pain.

Philosophically, this represents a fragmentation of the self: the body bears burden the conscious mind refuses to face.

Reclaiming these held emotions is a path toward reunifying fragmented aspects of being and reclaiming lost vitality.

Listening to the Body's Emotional Messages

A crucial step toward healing is cultivating the ability to listen deeply to bodily sensations without judgment or avoidance. This requires slowing down and developing somatic awareness—a mindful presence with physical experience.

Through practices like body scanning, mindful movement, or simply pausing to notice where tension resides, we begin to translate the body's silent language of emotion.

These listening honours the body's wisdom and fosters compassionate self-attunement.

Techniques for Releasing Stored Emotions

Once we recognize where emotions reside in the body, the next step is learning how to release them safely and effectively. Many modalities offer paths for this liberation:

- **Breathwork:** Deep, intentional breathing can dissolve muscular tension and facilitate emotional release.
- **Movement:** Dance, yoga, or simple stretching allow the body to express and discharge emotional energy.
- **Touch and Massage:** Therapeutic touch soothes muscle tightness and awakens sensory awareness.
- **Somatic Experiencing:** A therapeutic approach that helps gently unlock trauma stored in the body.
- **Vocalization:** Expressing emotions through sound, crying, or laughter helps free trapped energy.

Philosophically, these methods honour the body as a living, feeling entity, allowing emotion to complete its natural cycle.

The Role of Trauma and Emotional Storage

Trauma profoundly imprints on the body. Unlike ordinary emotions, trauma may freeze the body in protective patterns, causing deep muscular guarding or numbness.

Understanding trauma as an embodied experience shifts the healing process from solely mental analysis to a somatic journey. This requires patience, safety, and compassionate presence.

Recognizing the body's role in holding trauma offers hope for recovery through embodied awareness and release.

Embracing Vulnerability and Emotional Honesty

To access emotions stored in the body, one must embrace vulnerability—the willingness to feel without defense or denial.

This openness is an act of courage and self-friendship. It invites the soul's whisper to rise from the depths of flesh, healing old wounds and fostering authenticity.

Philosophically, vulnerability bridges the divide between isolation and connection, self and other, body and soul.

The Ethical Relationship with One's Own Body

Honouring the body's emotional wisdom requires cultivating an ethical relationship—one of respect, care, and attentive listening.

This relationship rejects harsh judgment or objectification and embraces the body as a sacred companion on the path of self-discovery.

Treating the body with kindness, patience, and gentleness creates fertile ground for emotional healing.

Integrating Emotional Awareness into Daily Life

Emotional embodiment is not reserved for special moments; it can permeate everyday living.

Small acts of mindfulness—pausing to check in with bodily sensations, breathing into discomfort, acknowledging feelings—create ongoing dialogue between body and soul.

Over time, this integration nurtures resilience, emotional clarity, and wholeness.

The Transformative Power of Emotional Release

Releasing stored emotion is a transformative act. It clears energetic blockages, reduces physical pain, and opens the heart.

Philosophically, this release is akin to shedding old skins, making room for renewed vitality and deeper presence.

It invites a reawakening of the body's natural fluidity and the soul's radiance.

Emotions as Teachers and Allies

Instead of enemies to be conquered or distractions to be avoided, emotions become teachers—guiding us toward unmet needs, unresolved wounds, or hidden desires.

By listening to where emotions live in the body, we learn to read their language and respond with compassion.

This relationship turns emotion into an ally for growth and healing.

Final Reflection: Reclaiming the Flesh as Home

To live fully is to live embodied. Emotions are not abstract forces but vibrant currents flowing through flesh and bone.

Reclaiming the body as home for emotions dissolves alienation and reconnects us to ourselves.

As body and soul reunite through awareness and release, we rediscover the profound friendship that sustains us until the end and beyond.

EIGHTEEN

PLEASURE WITHOUT GUILT

Pleasure—simple, profound, and often misunderstood—is a birthright of the body and soul. Yet, for many, it remains cloaked in layers of shame, guilt, or denial. This chapter is an invitation to reclaim pleasure as an essential and natural part of human existence. To reframe it not as a fleeting indulgence or a moral failing, but as a vital expression of our aliveness, intimacy, and connection.

Here, we explore the philosophy of pleasure, why guilt often shadows it, and how embracing pleasure without self-reproach restores harmony between body and soul. We journey through the cultural conditioning that distorts pleasure, examine the mind-body relationship, and discover how Honouring pleasure nourishes well-being, creativity, and the sacred dance of life.

The Nature of Pleasure: A Sacred Gift

Pleasure is more than mere gratification of the senses; it is an experience deeply woven into the fabric of life itself. Philosophers from the ancient Greeks to modern thinkers recognized pleasure's role not just as hedonistic delight, but as a path toward flourishing.

Aristotle called it *eudaimonia*—a flourishing life in which pleasure harmonizes with virtue and purpose. Pleasure, in its truest sense, is a signal from the body and soul that we are aligned with our own nature.

Whether it's the warmth of sunlight on skin, the tenderness of a loving touch, the rhythm of breath, or the joy of laughter, pleasure connects us to the present moment, to our senses, and ultimately to ourselves.

The Body's Innate Capacity for Pleasure

Our bodies are designed for pleasure. From the soothing comfort of a caress to the exhilaration of movement, pleasure is embedded in our nervous systems as a way to guide and nurture life.

Neuroscience confirms that pleasure activates reward pathways, releases feel-good chemicals like dopamine and endorphins, and supports emotional resilience.

Philosophically, the body is not a passive vessel but a dynamic participant in the dance of pleasure. To deny this aspect is to deny an essential part of our wholeness.

Cultural Conditioning: The Roots of Guilt

Despite pleasure's naturalness, many cultures—through religious, social, or moral teachings—have cast it as dangerous, sinful, or frivolous. This has created a powerful internalized voice of guilt, warning against indulgence and urging self-control, restraint, or even punishment.

This conditioning disconnects us from the wisdom of our bodies and from the soul's yearning for joy and connection. It creates a paradox: while we hunger for pleasure, we simultaneously reject it.

Guilt acts as a barrier, erecting walls between the body's desires and the soul's need for fulfilment.

The Mind-Body Split and Pleasure's Alienation

The historical separation of mind and body has contributed to the alienation of pleasure. The mind, seen as rational and serious, often judges and suppresses the body's sensual urges.

This split perpetuates shame around the body and its needs, framing pleasure as a weakness or distraction from higher purpose.

Reclaiming pleasure demands reintegrating mind and body, Honouring the body's messages as sacred, and allowing the soul to dance freely within the flesh.

Redefining Pleasure: Beyond the Physical

Pleasure is often reduced to purely physical sensations—food, sex, touch—but its true scope is broader.

Philosophically, pleasure encompasses emotional joy, intellectual satisfaction, creative flow, spiritual connection, and relational intimacy.

A sunset's beauty, a meaningful conversation, the completion of a creative work, or a moment of forgiveness can all evoke profound pleasure.

This expanded understanding opens pathways to experiencing pleasure that nourish the entire self.

The Relationship Between Pleasure and Intimacy

Pleasure and intimacy are intertwined. To experience pleasure fully, especially in relationships, requires vulnerability and presence.

Intimacy—whether with oneself or another—is the deep meeting of bodies, minds, and souls, where pleasure becomes a shared, sacred language.

When guilt infiltrates this space, it stifles authentic connection and diminishes the soul's capacity to receive and give joy.

Healing this relationship means embracing pleasure as a form of love and acceptance.

The Ethics of Pleasure: Consent, Respect, and Boundaries

Reclaiming pleasure without guilt does not mean abandoning ethics or responsibility.

True pleasure honours consent, respects boundaries, and arises from genuine desire rather than coercion or harm.

Philosophically, ethical pleasure is aligned with virtue, recognizing the dignity of self and others.

This balance cultivates pleasure as a force for healing, growth, and connection rather than domination or escape.

Reclaiming Pleasure: Practices for Embodiment

How can one reclaim pleasure in daily life? Here are some pathways grounded in embodiment and mindfulness:

- **Mindful Sensory Awareness:** Attuning to senses—taste, touch, sound, sight, smell—with full presence opens the gateway to pleasure.
- **Self-Touch and Massage:** Gentle touch reconnects us to the body's textures and feelings, inviting relaxation and joy.
- **Movement and Dance:** Moving freely honours the body's natural rhythms and awakens pleasure through expression.
- **Creative Expression:** Painting, music, writing—engaging creativity taps into pleasure beyond words.
- **Sacred Rest:** Allowing oneself rest without guilt honours the body's need for restoration and pleasure in stillness.
- **Intimate Connection:** Cultivating deep presence with loved ones opens channels for shared pleasure.

Pleasure and the Healing Journey

Pleasure is not merely a reward but an essential aspect of healing. Trauma, shame, and disconnection often suppress pleasure, locking it away behind walls of fear.

Healing involves rediscovering pleasure as a sign of safety and trust in oneself and the world.

Allowing oneself to experience pleasure becomes a radical act of reclaiming sovereignty over one's body and soul.

The Role of Joy as Resistance

In a culture that often glorifies busyness, achievement, and control, choosing pleasure can be an act of resistance.

Joy, laughter, and delight challenge the narratives of scarcity, fear, and guilt.

Philosophically, embracing pleasure is embracing abundance and the fullness of life itself.

It invites us to remember that to live fully is to savour the sweetness of being alive.

Navigating Guilt: Compassion and Relearning

Guilt may not vanish overnight. It often requires compassion, patience, and intentional relearning.

Recognizing guilt's origins—external messages, internalized judgments—allows one to disentangle from its grip.

Practices like journaling, therapy, or supportive communities create safe spaces to explore and release guilt around pleasure.

This journey is about reclaiming one's birthright gently and steadily.

The Unity of Body and Soul in Pleasure

Pleasure is a bridge connecting body and soul—a language where flesh speaks to spirit and spirit responds in kind.

When pleasure is embraced without guilt, the body becomes a temple of joy, and the soul sings in celebration.

This unity nourishes vitality, creativity, and a deep sense of belonging within oneself.

Final Reflection: Living a Life Rich with Pleasure

To live without guilt in pleasure is to live fully, authentically, and deeply connected.

It requires breaking free from old stories, Honouring the body's wisdom, and welcoming the soul's delight.

This chapter is an invitation to step into a life where pleasure is embraced as a sacred companion, a friend who walks with us to the end and beyond.

NINETEEN

GRATITUDE RITUALS FOR THE BODY

To walk this earth in a body is both a miracle and a mystery. We often forget this until illness or age reminds us of the fragility of our form. Yet, the body—our first and most faithful companion—carries us through every emotion, every encounter, every experience. It is the medium through which life unfolds. And yet, how rarely do we pause to say thank you?

This chapter is a sacred invitation to cultivate gratitude rituals for the body, not as grand gestures or fleeting affirmations, but as enduring practices of reverence. Gratitude is more than politeness; it is a form of intimacy. When expressed sincerely, it becomes a philosophical posture of respect and love toward the self. Through daily gratitude rituals, we can begin to heal the severance between mind and body, and between the self and the sacred.

The Philosophy of Gratitude

Gratitude, in its purest form, is a profound acknowledgment of being. It is an acceptance that we are held by something larger than ourselves—whether that be the cosmos, nature, or the simple breath of being alive. The Stoics practiced gratitude as a form of resilience; the Buddhists as a form of mindfulness; and mystics as a form of devotion.

When directed toward the body, gratitude transforms the body from object to sacred partner. We cease treating the body as something to fix or punish and begin Honouring it as something that serves, communicates, and feels.

Why Gratitude to the Body Matters

Gratitude for the body isn't about vanity or self-indulgence. It's about relationship. Many of us live estranged from our bodies, treating them as burdens or disappointments. We override fatigue, shame our appearances, and ignore signs of pain. This distance weakens the bond between soul and body, between consciousness and form.

Daily gratitude rituals can begin to restore that broken trust. They signal to the body: "I see you. I appreciate you. I will listen."

When the body feels seen, it relaxes. When it feels appreciated, it begins to respond with vitality. Gratitude awakens presence. Presence restores wholeness.

Morning Ritual: A Thank-You Upon Waking

Before reaching for a phone or listing tasks for the day, place a hand over your heart or belly and whisper a simple thank-you:

"Thank you, body, for another day. For the breath that sustains me. For the heart that beats without asking."

This simple pause sets the tone for a relationship of reverence throughout the day. The act of thanking the body upon waking reminds you that life is not guaranteed, and that every sensation, no matter how subtle, is a gift.

Touch as Gratitude

Touch can be a profound form of thankfulness. Rather than using touch to manipulate or correct the body, we can use it to affirm and acknowledge.

- **Massage**: A self-massage, even just a few minutes on shoulders or feet, is a tactile way to say: I care for you.
- **Lotioning the Skin**: Turn a daily routine into a ritual. As you apply lotion, do so mindfully, thanking each part: the hands that held, the legs that carried, the back that supported.

This is not about perfection, but presence. Let your touch communicate tenderness.

Breath as a Channel of Thanks

Breathing is the body's first offering of life. Yet it is often shallow, automatic, forgotten. Through conscious breath, we return to gratitude:

- Inhale: I receive.
- Exhale: I thank you.

Take a few minutes each day to breathe intentionally, letting your breath become a conversation with the body. With each inhale, acknowledge the energy the body provides. With each exhale, offer your gratitude back.

Gratitude Through Movement

Movement is not only exercise; it is an expression of vitality. Whether it's stretching, dancing, walking, or yoga, moving the body with awareness becomes a form of appreciation.

Try this ritual:

- Stand still, close your eyes, and say internally: "Thank you, feet, for grounding me."
- Begin to sway or move gently, acknowledging each part that participates: ankles, knees, hips, spine, shoulders.

Let your movement become prayer. It is not about performance but presence.

Eating with Reverence

Food is more than fuel—it is communion. Eating becomes a ritual when approached with gratitude:

- Thank the hands that prepared the food.
- Thank the body that will digest and nourish from it.
- Savor each bite without rushing.

This practice transforms eating from consumption to sacred exchange. It also deepens awareness of hunger and fullness, cultivating trust between you and your body's cues.

Evening Ritual: Reflective Thanks

As the day closes, take a few moments to thank your body for carrying you through:

"Thank you, eyes, for what you let me see. Thank you, arms, for embracing others. Thank you, voice, for speaking my truth."

Even on days of pain, illness, or fatigue, there is something to honour. Gratitude, especially in difficulty, becomes a radical act of compassion.

Writing a Letter to Your Body

One powerful ritual is writing a letter of gratitude to your body. Begin with:

"Dear Body, I'm sorry for... Thank you for... I promise to..."

This opens a deeper dialogue, allowing hidden feelings to surface and healing to begin.

You may discover emotions—grief, forgiveness, joy—that have been locked in the tissues of your being. Let the letter be honest and sacred.

The Alchemy of Gratitude

Gratitude does not require perfection. You don't need to wait until your body looks a certain way or feels a certain way to be thankful. In fact, gratitude is most transformative when it is unconditional.

In this way, gratitude becomes alchemy. It turns shame into honour, fatigue into reverence, and disconnection into unity. It returns you to yourself—not as a project to be improved, but as a beloved to be cherished.

A Daily Ritual Sample

Morning (5 minutes)

- Place a hand on heart. Whisper thanks.
- Three deep breaths: Inhale (receive), Exhale (thank).

Midday (5 minutes)

- Stretch or walk slowly.
- Thank each part involved in movement.

Evening (5 minutes)

- Reflect on the body's support during the day.
- Write one line in a gratitude journal: "Today my body helped me..."

Over time, these small acts weave a larger pattern of love.

Gratitude as a Return Home

Ultimately, gratitude rituals are not about adding more to your day but about remembering. They are invitations to come home—to the skin, the breath, the heartbeat that never left you.

When you thank your body, you are not only healing it—you are also healing the fractured sense of self that forgot it was already whole.

In the echo of every thank-you lives the whisper of something eternal: I am here. I am grateful. I am enough.

Would you like me to continue with Chapter 20 or explore a specific practice from this chapter in more depth?

TWENTY

YOUR BODY IS ON YOUR SIDE

The relationship we share with our body is often misunderstood. We tend to view it as a tool to be disciplined, a vehicle to be shaped, or a nuisance when pain arises. Rarely do we pause to acknowledge the body as an ally—a steadfast companion that has walked every step of our life's journey beside us. This chapter, the final in Part II, invites a fundamental shift: from suspicion to trust, from criticism to reverence. It is a return to the awareness that our body is, and always has been, on our side.

The Unseen Work of the Body

From the moment of our first breath to the stillness of our final one, our body performs countless functions without our instruction or awareness. The heart beats with unwavering rhythm, lungs expand and contract, skin heals from wounds, and the immune system battles unseen invaders. Even when we sleep, the body works tirelessly to restore, detoxify, and regenerate.

This silent orchestration is not accidental—it is devotion. The body is not merely a mechanical structure but a deeply intelligent organism working in favour of life. Even fatigue is a favour. Pain is a signal. Hunger is a guide. All these are its ways of communicating care and calling us back to equilibrium.

When we begin to see our body as a messenger rather than a betrayer, everything changes. We stop punishing it and start listening. We begin to nourish instead of neglect, to rest instead of override, and to thank instead of blame.

Pain as Protection

We often label pain as the enemy. But pain is one of the body's clearest voices. It doesn't rise up to ruin our lives—it emerges to preserve them. Pain says: something needs attention. Something must be changed.

Consider a headache. It might be asking us to rest. A stomachache may urge us to reconsider what we consume. Chronic tension could reflect prolonged stress or emotional repression. Instead of silencing these symptoms with pills and distractions, what if we treated them like alarm bells from a devoted guardian?

The body doesn't betray us with pain; it protects us by warning us. It shows us where we are living out of alignment—physically, emotionally, or spiritually. The aches, the fatigue, the inflammation, the disease—they are not punishments but pleas for kindness, pauses for reflection, calls for healing.

The Weight, We Ask It to Carry

Beyond the biological, our body carries emotional weight—trauma, grief, shame, and unspoken fear. These don't just live in our mind; they lodge in our muscles, settle in our chest, twist in our gut. When the soul cannot express its truth, the body will carry it. It does not judge our wounds; it simply holds them, waiting for us to acknowledge and release them.

And it doesn't stop functioning. Even under emotional storms, physical neglect, and critical stares, it continues—loyally, patiently. This is not weakness. It is deep strength. The body loves us in a language too subtle for words but too persistent to ignore.

Trusting the Body Again

To live a life of wholeness, we must begin to trust our body again. Trust it to tell the truth. Trust it to know what it needs. Trust it to alert us when we're off track.

This is not blind obedience but conscious partnership. You don't surrender your will to the body, but you enter into dialogue. You ask, you listen, you respond with respect.

When you feel the pull of fatigue, instead of pushing harder, you soften. When you sense hunger, you explore what your body truly needs. When you feel tightness in your chest, you ask: what emotion is asking to be seen? You become a friend to the body, not a commander.

Rewriting the Narrative

Many of us grew up in systems—cultural, educational, religious—that trained us to override the body. We were told to sit still, ignore pain, hide emotion, and keep moving. We learned to view the body as sinful, shameful, or untrustworthy. These inherited narratives run deep, shaping how we relate to our physical form.

But we have the power to rewrite them. To reclaim the body as sacred. To see its curves, scars, and signals as beautiful. To stop waging war against the very form that houses our spirit.

The moment we choose to see the body as a friend is the moment healing begins. Because friendship requires respect, compassion, and presence. It doesn't require perfection.

The Power of Simple Acts

The body doesn't demand grand gestures. It asks for consistency, not extravagance. A stretch in the morning. A warm meal when hunger strikes. Breath when stress tightens the chest. Water. Rest. A kind word whispered in front of a mirror.

These small acts restore trust. They remind the body it is not abandoned. And slowly, the body begins to soften, open, and respond. Health improves. Vitality returns. Inner dialogue transforms. You feel safer—because you are safe with yourself.

Unity: No Separation Between Body and Self

Too often, we say things like, "my body is failing me," or "I hate my thighs," or "my back is killing me." These are not harmless thoughts—they reflect a fractured relationship. They assume a separation where there is none. You are not in a body—you are your body. And when you speak unkindly to it, you are speaking unkindly to yourself.

To restore wholeness, we must collapse this illusion of separation. Begin to speak to your body as you would a child, a dear friend, or a beloved companion. Even when it's hurting. Especially when it's hurting.

This is the essence of embodiment—not just living in the body, but with it. As one. With awareness, kindness, and unity.

The Return to Self-Companionship

In the quiet moments—when the noise fades, the demands pause, and the masks come off—you are left with yourself. Your breath. Your heartbeat. Your presence.

It is here that the deepest friendship is born. A bond that cannot be broken by external failures or achievements. A loyalty untouched by changing appearances. A love not based on performance but on being.

Your body never left you. Not when you ignored it. Not when you punished it. Not when you forgot its needs. It kept showing up—every day—on your side.

So now, maybe it's time you show up for it. With gentleness. With reverence. With love.

This is the pact of embodiment: I am on my side. I walk with myself. I honour my form. I listen when it speaks. I rest when it's tired. I thank it when it serves. I love it because it is mine—and because it is me.

Let this be the beginning of a new chapter. One where you no longer fight the body, ignore its cries, or deny its wisdom. One where you return to yourself—to the sacred partnership you've always had, whether you realized it or not.

Because the body has always been with you. Because the body has always been on your side.

TWENTY-ONE

THE SOUL IS NOT A CONCEPT

Deepening the Relationship with the Inner Self

To speak of the soul is to tread into a realm often relegated to mystics, poets, and philosophers. It is frequently treated as a metaphor, a vague abstraction, or a religious token to be acknowledged but not necessarily embraced. Yet, what if we stepped back and looked again? What if we realized that the soul is not a distant, elusive idea but a living, breathing presence that animates us from within—patient, watchful, and ever yearning for connection?

The soul is not a concept. It is your essence. It is the thread of continuity between who you are today and who you were before language gave shape to thought. It is the silent witness to every moment you have lived, every joy you've held, and every wound you carry. To ignore it is to turn from your own heartbeat, to silence a voice that never ceases to speak, even when you refuse to listen.

Our modern world tends to compartmentalize. The body becomes something to shape, the mind something to sharpen, and the soul—if acknowledged at all—is something to ponder in quiet hours, often only in times of crisis. But such division is artificial. The soul is not a compartment. It is the very glue of our being, the core that unites body, mind, and spirit. Without the soul, we are fractured. With the soul, we become whole.

From a philosophical lens, the soul has long fascinated thinkers. Plato believed the soul was immortal, a divine essence that descended into a mortal body. Aristotle saw it as the animating principle of life. Eastern traditions, too, hold the soul as central—called Atman in Hinduism, the spark of universal consciousness, or in Buddhism, approached through mindfulness and awareness of suffering, even if the concept of an eternal self is debated. Regardless of the framework, the soul is never dismissed; it is revered.

But philosophy alone cannot grasp the soul. It must be felt. You sense it in the quiet pull toward meaning, in the moments of awe that stop your breath, in the quiet resistance you feel when your life veers away from truth. The soul speaks not in grand declarations but in gentle murmurs, the kind that stir your intuition and ask you to pause, to reconsider, to listen.

The soul is experienced most vividly in the spaces between actions—in silence, in reflection, in heartbreak, and in love. It is the part of you that weeps not because you are weak but because you are deeply alive. It is the voice that says, "There is more to this life," even when you seem to have all you need. It is the ache in your chest when you betray yourself, the subtle joy when you return to your centre.

When we treat the soul as a concept, we strip it of its power. We make it a thing to be debated rather than lived. But when we begin to see it as an intimate friend—a wise, patient, compassionate presence that has always been with us—we begin to shift. We start showing up differently. We speak more kindly to ourselves. We take pauses to breathe. We begin to ask not just, "What do I want?" but also, "What does my soul need?"

The soul is not separate from the body. It resides within it, moves through it, and expresses itself through its rhythms. When your body is tired, it is your soul asking for restoration. When your heart feels heavy, it is your soul asking to be heard. To live a soulful life is not to escape the world but to engage with it more deeply, more truthfully.

One of the greatest tragedies of modern life is the pressure to silence the soul. We are told to be efficient, to move quickly, to chase productivity. The soul, on the other hand, demands slowness. It thrives in spaciousness. It blooms in stillness. It asks us to savour rather than rush, to witness rather than conquer, to dwell in presence rather than escape into distraction.

And so many of us numb ourselves—not because we are weak, but because we are aching. When the soul is silenced for too long, its quiet whispers become sharp pains. Emptiness sets in. We start to feel as though something essential is missing, even if we cannot name it. That emptiness is not a flaw; it is an invitation. It is your soul asking you to come home.

To honour the soul is to befriend yourself on the deepest level. It is to say, "I will no longer abandon the part of me that knows." It is to respect your longings, your fears, your questions, and your dreams. It is to hold space for your wounds, not as evidence of failure but as proof that you have lived.

How do you connect with the soul? Not through force, but through invitation. You listen. You journal. You walk without your phone. You sit under the sky. You engage in rituals that matter to you, even if they are as simple as lighting a candle or listening to a song that moves you. You reflect on your experiences, not just with the mind but with the heart.

The more you listen, the louder the soul becomes. The more you honour its wisdom, the more your life begins to feel aligned. Decisions become clearer. Relationships become more authentic. You begin to live in harmony with your values, not just your obligations. And most importantly, you feel less alone—because you are finally walking with yourself, soul intact.

You don't need to believe in any particular religion or doctrine to acknowledge the soul. You need only to believe in the sacredness of your own experience. You need only to recognize that within you lives something unmeasurable yet deeply real. Something that seeks beauty, that yearns for love, that aches for purpose. That something is your soul.

In a world that tempts you to live on the surface, choosing to engage with your soul is an act of rebellion. It is a declaration that your life is not just a series of tasks but a sacred unfolding. It is a way of saying, "I matter—not because of what I produce, but because of who I am."

The soul is not a concept. It is you.

Let that truth settle.

Let it guide you.

And from that place, may you begin to live not just more fully—but more soulfully.

TWENTY-TWO
Signs of a Soul Disconnected

There is no wound more subtle than the quiet rupture between a human being and their own soul. It does not scream, it does not bleed, and rarely does it make itself visible in ways others can see. Yet it corrodes from within—softly, consistently, like wind hollowing out a stone cliff over centuries. A disconnected soul does not announce its absence. It simply withdraws, waiting patiently for you to notice.

This chapter is not about despair, though it may pass through it. It is about recognition. For to recognize disconnection is the first whisper of return.

1. The Numbness That Grows Without Reason

There comes a day—perhaps many—when you wake and feel... nothing. Not joy, not sorrow. Just a greyness, not painted on the world, but soaked into your very being. The world continues: birds still sing, people still smile, the sky still moves through its majestic cycle. But none of it stirs you. And perhaps worse—you don't mind.

Numbness is often misunderstood. It is not peace, though it can mimic it. It is not quietude, though it can feel like silence. True peace is alive, attentive, vibrant even in stillness. Numbness is the opposite: a retreat of vitality. The soul has begun to shield itself from a world it no longer trusts.

Why does this happen? Sometimes, the mind becomes too full of noise, expectations, or trauma, and the soul—delicate yet deep—chooses to mute itself for protection. The numbness is not the absence of feeling but the soul's refusal to be wounded further.

To awaken from numbness, we must not demand emotion, but offer safety. We must create silence not filled with screens or stimulation, but with room for the soul to breathe again.

2. The Weight of Apathy

Apathy is not laziness; it is disinterest born from disorientation. When you begin to ask, "What's the point?" and no longer seek the answer—it is a sign. When once-loved passions fade and no new fires take their place, the soul is no longer being nourished.

We live in a world obsessed with purpose and productivity. But the soul does not speak in deadlines or resumes. It speaks in meaning, in resonance. Apathy creeps in when the actions of life become detached from the essence of life.

You may still be doing what you've always done—working, talking, moving—but feel as though you're watching someone else's story. Apathy is the soul whispering: *this is not your path.* Or perhaps: *you have forgotten why you chose it.*

The answer is not always to quit everything. Sometimes, the smallest shift—a walk at dawn, a conversation with a tree, a song remembered from childhood—can reawaken the thread of connection.

3. Disconnection in a Crowded Room

You are surrounded by people. Friends laugh nearby. A party, a celebration, a workplace full of chatter. And yet, you feel utterly alone. Not just socially—but spiritually. You might be smiling, even charming. But inside, you are on a distant shore.

Disconnection can happen even when everything appears fine. This is perhaps its most insidious form. You may not even realize it until the silence between thoughts becomes unbearable.

When the soul disconnects, it often withdraws from the illusion. That is, the illusion of connection that lacks depth, honesty, or true presence. You might be talking, but not seen. Listened to, but not heard. Known, but not understood.

To heal this, seek out realness. Conversations without masks. Silence shared without awkwardness. Presence that asks nothing in return. One true connection can begin to call the soul back.

4. The Loss of Meaning

Meaning is the light by which the soul navigates the world. When meaning begins to fade, life itself can start to feel like a stage play that no longer makes sense. You know your lines, but they sound hollow. You know your role, but it no longer fits.

Sometimes, this happens gradually—like colour draining from a photograph. Other times, it's abrupt: a loss, a betrayal, a moment that breaks the narrative you once believed in. The danger here is not in the change of meaning, but in the belief that no new meaning can arise.

Meaning is not static. It is not a singular answer written in stone. It is a dialogue—a conversation between your soul and the world. When the conversation stops, the soul retreats.

But even in this void, meaning waits to be rediscovered. Perhaps in art. Perhaps in service. Perhaps in silence itself. Begin not with the big questions—but with the small ones: *What moved me today? What made me pause?* From there, the roots begin to grow again.

5. A Strange Homesickness

It is entirely possible to feel homesick while standing in your own house. To feel like a stranger in your own skin. This sense of being "out of place" is not always geographical. Often, it is existential. You are not where your soul longs to be.

This homesickness is the soul's compass pointing toward something forgotten—perhaps a path abandoned, a calling left behind, a version of yourself silenced by necessity or fear.

You may not know what you long for. But the longing itself is a sacred clue. Do not numb it. Do not dismiss it. Follow it gently, as one might follow birdsong through a forest. The path back to your soul may be winding, but the ache is your first guide.

6. The Endless Seeking of Substitutes

When the soul disconnects, the self begins to seek substitutes. We chase experiences, possessions, titles, distractions—not because we truly want them, but because we're trying to fill a space we cannot name.

Food, fame, romance, stimulation, endless scrolling, compulsive goals—all can become attempts to bridge the void. But none satisfy for long. And so the hunger returns.

This is not a call for asceticism. The soul is not against pleasure or beauty. But it does not thrive on substitutes. It hungers for depth, authenticity, presence. When we feed it surface-level stimulation, it remains unsatisfied.

To shift, ask not *what do I want to consume?* but *what do I long to create?* Not *what do I need to distract me?* but *what truth am I avoiding?*

7. A Life of Reaction, Not Intention

When the soul is disconnected, life becomes reactive. You wake up and immediately respond—to emails, demands, noise. Days pass in blur. You begin to feel that life is something happening *to* you, rather than something you are living from within.

This disconnection from intentionality is subtle but profound. The soul, when connected, brings with it a sense of sovereignty. Not control, but participation. You feel your choices matter. You feel yourself inside time, not just running from it.

To restore this, pause. Before action, sit in stillness. Even five minutes a day. Ask: *What is needed? What is true?* Let the soul have room to speak before the world begins to shout.

8. Doubting Your Own Voice

Perhaps the most heartbreaking sign of disconnection is when you no longer trust your own voice. You defer to others, second-guess yourself, or drown in the noise of competing opinions. The soul's voice grows faint—not because it is weak, but because it is quiet. And we have trained ourselves to value the loud.

Yet the soul does not argue. It does not compete. It waits.

To hear it again, begin to honour your intuition. Notice the way your body responds to situations. Reclaim solitude not as loneliness, but as the sacred space where your inner voice can speak freely.

The soul's wisdom does not come as certainty, but as a deep knowing. A stillness beneath thought. Trust it—not blindly, but gently. Let it grow by listening.

The Gentle Return

Disconnection is not failure. It is not weakness. It is not a punishment. It is a message—a sacred one.

To be disconnected is to be human. But to remain disconnected is a choice. And so, we are invited, again and again, to return.

This return does not require a grand transformation. It begins with attention. With sitting by a window and noticing how the light falls. With journaling your thoughts without judgment. With walking without headphones. With asking yourself not *what should I do?* but *what do I feel?*

The soul does not ask for perfection. It asks for presence.

Let the numbness be a bell. Let the apathy be a compass. Let the silence be a doorway. Let the homesickness guide you home—not to a place, but to a state of being where you are no longer alien to yourself.

The truth is, your soul has never left. It is not lost. It is waiting—for you to look inward, to listen, and to remember that beneath the noise, beneath the roles, beneath the doubt—there is something timeless and sacred, and it is you.

TWENTY-THREE

THE SOUL SPEAKS IN SILENCE

In a world filled with noise, urgency, and endless distraction, silence is often mistaken for emptiness. Yet silence is not void—it is a vessel. It holds the soul's language, the subtle frequencies of your deepest self, the quiet callings that cannot survive in the clangour of daily life. If you are seeking your soul, do not look first to books, voices, or even rituals. First, seek silence.

The soul rarely speaks in words. It reveals itself through sensations, symbols, longings, and dreams. In silence, it does not shout; it unfolds. Like a lotus blooming only in still water, the soul shows its face when you no longer chase the reflection, but sit beside it.

This chapter is a return to that ancient and sacred space—the temple of inner quiet where your truest self begins to whisper once again.

1. The Sacred Stillness of Silence

Silence is not merely the absence of sound. It is the presence of listening. In silence, everything that has been buried begins to surface—not to torment, but to be heard, to be known, and ultimately, to be integrated.

Many fear silence because they believe it will confront them with their pain. And yes, at first, it often does. The mind, long used to distractions, releases its stored griefs, regrets, or unresolved emotions. But beyond this surface turbulence lies a deeper stillness—a realm where insight dawns not as thought, but as truth recognized.

To sit in silence is to give the soul room to breathe. It is a return to the womb of consciousness, where you can remember who you are without the world's constant narration.

Start small. A few minutes each morning. No phone. No music. Just presence. In time, the silence will stop being empty. It will become intimate.

2. Solitude as a Gateway, not a Cage

Solitude is often misunderstood as loneliness. But solitude is not the absence of others; it is the presence of yourself. Loneliness is the ache of disconnection. Solitude is the embrace of wholeness.

When you retreat into solitude willingly, you enter a sacred space where the soul can rise to the surface. There are no roles to play, no masks to wear, no one to impress. In solitude, the self begins to unfold in its most natural state.

Think of great visionaries, poets, mystics—they all understood the value of stepping away, of going into the wilderness, into monasteries, into deserts, into forests. Not to escape the world, but to hear something deeper than the world's noise.

Solitude can be as simple as an hour alone in a room without distraction. Or a walk through trees without speaking. It's in these quiet sanctuaries that your soul, no longer pressured to perform, can start to hum again.

3. The Soul's Language of Dreams

Each night, as your conscious mind rests, the soul takes the stage. Not bound by logic or chronology, it speaks in symbols, metaphors, and mysteries. Dreams are not random—they are expressions of the unconscious, which is the soul's domain.

In dreams, your soul might appear as a forgotten house, a vast ocean, a wounded animal, or a brilliant star. The logic of dreams is not linear but intuitive. That is why they are often dismissed—because they do not conform to the structures of waking thought. But if you learn to listen, they will reveal what your waking self has missed.

Keep a dream journal. Not to analyse mechanically, but to notice patterns, images, and emotions. Ask: *What part of me is trying to speak through this? What truth am I avoiding? What desire have I ignored?*

The dreamscape is the soul's playground. It is also its sanctuary. Do not rush to interpret. Sit with your dreams. Let them ripen over time. In doing so, you may recover long-forgotten parts of yourself.

4. The Presence Behind the Breath

One of the simplest ways to return to your soul is through the breath. The breath is the bridge between body and spirit, the constant rhythm that accompanies every emotion, every thought, every silence.

When you follow your breath—not to control it, but to observe it—you enter a space beneath thought. This is where the soul begins to surface. It doesn't come as a voice from outside, but a feeling from within: the sense of being held, grounded, alive.

Many spiritual traditions centre their practices on breathwork for this reason. When you breathe consciously, you enter the now—and the soul only speaks in the now. It has no interest in your past victories or future fears. It wants to meet you here, exactly as you are.

So, pause. Inhale. Exhale. Do it again. And again. And soon, you will feel it—not a lightning bolt, but a gentle presence. Your soul, saying: *I'm here. I've always been here.*

5. The Importance of Sacred Pauses

Modern life teaches momentum, but the soul values stillness. If your life is a sentence, the soul lives in the punctuation—the commas, the pauses, the silences between syllables.

A sacred pause might be a cup of tea sipped slowly in the afternoon sun. It might be a moment of stillness before answering a question. It might be the decision to do nothing for an hour, just to see what arises.

When you practice these sacred pauses, you interrupt the trance of automatic living. And in that interruption, truth can emerge.

Ask yourself during a pause: *What is arising now? What am I being called to feel, to see, to release?*

The answers may not come in words. They may come as warmth, or tears, or peace. That is the soul, gently speaking.

6. The Wisdom in Nature's Silence

There is a reason why the ancient sages, prophets, and poets sought silence in nature. The trees do not hurry. The mountains do not speak. Yet something in their presence rearranges us. The silence of the natural world is not empty—it is full of knowing.

When you sit by a river and say nothing, something in you is heard. When you lie beneath the stars and ask no questions, some part of you receives answers. Not literal ones, but a shift in being.

Nature does not require you to be anyone. In its presence, you are permitted to simply be. And that permission is powerful. It allows the layers of ego and identity to fall away, revealing the essence beneath.

So go. Not to hike or photograph or achieve—but simply to be still. To walk slowly. To breathe with the trees. To listen—not with ears, but with your soul.

7. Letting Go of the Need for Words

There is a moment in the journey when words become insufficient. When you begin to feel things that cannot be explained, only experienced. This is not a failure of language. It is a deepening of awareness.

The soul does not rely on language. It communicates through presence, intuition, resonance. And sometimes, the truest thing you can do is sit in silence and allow what is, without needing to name it.

Let the silence do its work. Let it cleanse you of narratives that no longer serve. Let it hold you like a mother holds a child—without needing to fix, change, or explain.

In this space beyond words, healing happens.

8. When Silence Feels Empty—Wait Longer

There will be moments when silence feels unbearable. When solitude feels like exile. When dreams offer no answers. In these moments, many turn back—seeking noise, distraction, stimulation.

But if you can stay a little longer—just a moment longer—you may find that the silence was not empty. It was simply waiting for your full attention.

The soul does not perform on command. It waits for sincerity. For patience. For surrender. When you meet it there—not with expectation, but with openness—it begins to stir.

So stay. In the silence. In the pause. In the waiting. There is something being born in that quiet. And it is you.

9. The Return of Inner Music

Eventually, something shifts. Slowly, gently. You begin to feel an inner music returning. It may not be dramatic. It may come as a subtle hum, a lightness, a moment of awe at sunlight through leaves.

This is your soul reawakening. Not in noise, but in presence. You feel connected again—to yourself, to life, to something greater. You do not need to define it. It is enough to feel it.

That music is not outside you. It *is* you. It is the deep rhythm of your being when you are in harmony with truth, purpose, love.

And it was always there—waiting for you to fall silent enough to hear it.

Conclusion: The Sacred Language of Quiet

Silence, solitude, and dreams are not escapes. They are bridges. They lead not away from life, but into its heart. They do not make you less connected to others, but more deeply connected to yourself—and from that centre, all relationships deepen.

To walk the soul's path is to honour silence not as absence, but as presence. To seek solitude not as separation, but as union. To dream not as fantasy, but as sacred revelation.

In a world addicted to volume, those who cultivate quiet become rare beacons. Their wisdom comes not from what they say, but from the depth they carry in their silence.

You do not need to retreat forever. But you must retreat sometimes. Into the silence where the soul lives. Into the solitude where the self listens. Into the dreams where truth is clothed in symbol.

And there, in that quiet temple within, the soul will speak. Not with noise. Not with certainty. But with truth so pure it humbles you. With love so old it feels like remembering. And with guidance so subtle, it turns your whole life toward meaning again.

Sit with the silence. Honour it. And in time, it will sing.

TWENTY-FOUR
INTUITION IS INNER KNOWING

We often speak of intuition as a vague whisper, a hunch, or a sudden flash of insight. It comes unannounced, with no logic or explanation, yet we feel its certainty. Sometimes it urges us to go left when the road seems easier to the right. Sometimes it tells us to trust a stranger, walk away from comfort, or say yes before reason catches up. And more often than not, when we listen to this voice—this subtle, wordless guidance—we later realize we knew the truth long before we could explain it.

That is intuition: the soul speaking without words.

In this chapter, we will explore the sacred ground of inner knowing. We will not reduce intuition to superstition or impulse. Instead, we will honour it as one of the most profound expressions of soul-wisdom—a compass that exists not outside, but within. A compass that, when tuned and trusted, leads us home.

1. The Nature of Intuition

Intuition is not learned. It is remembered.

Every human being is born with intuitive knowing. Children use it effortlessly. They know whom to trust. They sense joy or tension in a room. They follow their wonder without asking for permission. They have not yet buried their inner knowing beneath layers of fear, logic, and social expectation.

But as we grow, we are taught to abandon this inner compass. We are told to rely on facts, to analyse, to justify. Feelings become suspect. Gut instincts are dismissed as irrational. And so, over time, our connection to the inner voice fades—not because it stops speaking, but because we stop listening.

Yet the voice remains. It waits. It appears in dreams, in sudden clarity, in goosebumps, in warnings we can't explain. It nudges us when something feels off, even if everything appears fine. It encourages us toward paths that feel right, even when they don't make sense to others.

The soul's wisdom is not loud. It does not demand. It offers. And that offering is intuition.

2. How the Soul Speaks Through Intuition

The soul does not argue. It does not debate. It reveals.

Intuition is the quiet unfolding of truth, a resonance in the heart before it reaches the mind. It bypasses logic not because it defies it, but because it comes from a deeper place—a place beneath thought.

It might come as:

- A sudden sense of clarity when you meet someone for the first time.
- A quiet unease that doesn't fade no matter how much you try to reason it away.
- A gentle pull toward a direction, a person, or a choice, with no evidence to support it.
- A dream that lingers, carrying meaning that words can't quite touch.
- A bodily sensation—tightness in the chest, warmth in the belly, tingling at the fingertips.

These are not accidents. They are the soul's signals. The question is: do you trust them?

3. The Distinction Between Intuition and Fear

One of the most common difficulties people face is differentiating between intuition and fear. Both can feel strong.

Both can urge or warn. So how do you tell the difference?

Fear is loud. Intuition is quiet.

Fear shouts in urgency. Intuition speaks with clarity.

Fear is rooted in past wounds or future projections. Intuition is anchored in the present.

Fear contracts your energy. Intuition expands it.

When you feel fear, it is often accompanied by tension, pressure, and racing thoughts. When you feel intuition, there is often a sense of peace—even if the message it carries is challenging.

To develop discernment, pause before reacting. Ask yourself: *Is this arising from a wound or from wisdom?* Fear demands reaction. Intuition invites response.

4. Reawakening the Intuitive Mind

To reconnect with your inner knowing, you must slow down. The intuitive voice cannot be heard in a rush. It is not designed to compete with noise.

Here are gentle practices to reawaken your intuitive mind:

1. Daily Stillness: Begin each day with five minutes of silence. Just sit. Breathe. Notice. Over time, you'll recognize your soul's texture—its subtle whispers beneath thought.

2. Body Awareness: Your body is a tuning fork for truth. When making a decision, close your eyes and feel into it. Does it bring contraction or expansion? Anxiety or calm?

3. Dream Journaling: Write down your dreams upon waking. Over time, patterns emerge. You begin to recognize when the soul is using dream-symbols to send guidance.

4. Nature Connection: Spend time in the natural world. Walk without headphones. Observe the movements of animals, the flow of water, the stillness of trees. Nature helps realign your inner compass.

5. Ask and Listen: Ask your soul questions. "What is right for me?" "What am I not seeing?" Then don't force the answer. Wait. Be receptive. The answer may come later—in a word, a feeling, a coincidence.

5. Trusting What You Know Without Proof

One of the greatest acts of spiritual maturity is learning to trust what you know before the world confirms it.

You may feel something is wrong in a relationship, even if everything looks perfect. You may feel called to a path others dismiss. You may feel a deep pull away from something that "makes sense" and toward something unknown.

Trust it.

You do not need external permission to honour your inner knowing. It is enough that *you know*. Your soul is your truest authority. And though the world may not always validate your choices, your life will.

It takes courage to walk by intuition. But every time you do, you strengthen that muscle. You remember: *I have always known. I had simply forgotten to listen.*

6. When Intuition Leads to the Unknown

Intuition does not promise comfort. It promises truth.

Sometimes the soul will lead you away from safety and toward uncertainty—not to punish, but to awaken. You may feel called to leave a job, speak a truth, or say goodbye. These moments are not easy. But they are sacred.

You are not meant to understand the full map. Intuition offers only the next step. That is enough. Life unfolds in response to each step taken in truth.

So when you feel the nudge, the pull, the knowing—follow. Even if it makes no sense. Especially then. Intuition is not about predicting the future. It's about Honouring the present.

7. Intuition in Relationships

In the realm of relationships, intuition is indispensable. It tells you when something feels aligned, when someone is not being fully honest, or when a connection is meant to be more—or less—than what it appears.

Many stay in relationships because they ignore that inner knowing. "They haven't done anything wrong," they say. "Maybe it's just me." But often, it *isn't* just you. It is the soul revealing what your eyes cannot yet see.

When you meet someone new, notice your first feeling. Not just attraction—but resonance. How does your body feel in their presence? At ease? Guarded? Uplifted?

The soul recognizes energy. Long before the mind rationalizes, the heart already knows. Trust it.

8. Intuition as Creative Compass

Artists, musicians, writers, inventors—all draw from the well of intuition. The creative act is not the product of pure intellect, but of surrender. It is a dance with the unknown.

When you trust your intuition, you enter the flow. You allow something greater than your conscious mind to guide your hand. Ideas come, not through effort, but through openness.

To live creatively is to live intuitively. It means listening not only for what is logical, but for what is alive.

9. Strengthening the Inner Voice

Like any relationship, your connection with intuition deepens through trust and attention. Here are ways to strengthen it:

- **Act on small knowings.** Don't wait for huge decisions. Start by listening to what food your body wants, which road you feel like walking, which book calls you. These micro-choices build trust.
- **Track your intuitive hits.** Write down moments when you felt something before it happened. This will reveal your inner pattern.
- **Reduce noise.** Intuition doesn't compete with constant input. Limit excessive media, gossip, overthinking. Create quiet inside and out.
- **Forgive your past dismissals.** We've all ignored intuition and paid a price. But guilt doesn't help. Learn from it. Move forward wiser.

10. Living Guided by Inner Knowing

To live by intuition is not to abandon logic or reason. It is to let the soul lead, and the mind support.

This means trusting that your life knows how to unfold. That you do not have to figure everything out. That you can let go of the obsession with control and begin to flow with the deeper current within.

It means understanding that your purpose, your truth, your path—they are not things you must invent. They are things you must remember. They are revealed through listening.

Intuition is not a luxury. It is not a gift reserved for mystics or empaths. It is a birthright. It is the soul's way of guiding you through the mystery of living with grace.

Conclusion: The Voice You've Always Known

There is a voice inside you that has never been wrong. Perhaps you didn't hear it clearly, or perhaps you ignored it. But it was there, steady, quiet, waiting.

It is the voice that nudged you away from danger, led you toward unexpected joys, kept you from betrayals you didn't yet understand. It is the voice that reminded you who you were when you felt lost.

This voice is not a stranger. It is your soul.

To live in harmony with your soul is to make space for this voice daily. Not just in crisis, but in calm. Not just when confused, but also when grateful.

The more you listen, the louder it becomes. The more you trust, the clearer it speaks. Until one day, you realize: you no longer need to seek guidance. Because guidance is who you are.

Your soul is not somewhere else. It is not silent. It is speaking now. Can you hear it?

TWENTY-FIVE
SOUL LOSS AND SOUL RETRIEVAL

There are times in life when we feel as though something essential has slipped through our fingers—quietly, silently, without notice. It may not announce itself with chaos, but rather with a subtle emptiness, a loss of vitality, a dull ache where our spirit once danced. This sensation, though often unnamed, is not rare. It is the echo of what ancient traditions have long referred to as *soul loss*.

What Is Soul Loss?

Soul loss is not merely a poetic metaphor—it is a spiritual and psychological truth felt in the deep interior of our being. It refers to those moments, often following trauma, betrayal, grief, or sustained neglect, where a part of our essence withdraws for survival. In childhood, this may occur through emotional abandonment or abuse; in adulthood, through loss, heartbreak, or chronic emotional suppression. We fracture in order to survive.

This part of the soul—the energy, clarity, or joy that once animated us—doesn't vanish. It retreats. It waits, often silently, until the day we become still enough, gentle enough, brave enough to call it back.

In modern psychology, this is echoed in the concept of dissociation. When pain is too overwhelming, the mind partitions it away. In ancient shamanic traditions, this is described as the soul leaving the body during a moment of great distress. The language differs, but the core truth remains: the self protects itself by turning inward, by closing a door.

How Do We Recognize Soul Loss?

Soul loss does not always scream. Sometimes it merely hums.

You may feel it in persistent numbness—the inability to cry, even when tears are appropriate. Or in the haunting sensation that you're observing life from the outside, disconnected from purpose or passion. You may sense that you're living someone else's story, your voice barely audible within your own life. Chronic fatigue, apathy, or a longing that cannot be named may all be signs that something within has gone missing.

It is the sense of being homesick, but not knowing where home is.

You might forget what it feels like to be fully alive—to laugh without effort, to dance without self-consciousness, to speak without shrinking. You might find yourself unable to trust, to love deeply, or to remain in the present moment without fear. These are not just emotional difficulties. They are often signals of soul fragments left behind in moments of great wounding.

The Causes: Trauma, Betrayal, and Abandonment

Soul loss is often seeded in trauma. When something hurts us so deeply that we cannot hold it all, our soul retreats. Children, in particular, are vulnerable. In their innocence, they might internalize the cruelty of others as proof that they themselves are unworthy. A child who is shamed for expressing emotion may send away the part of themselves that feels. A child who is neglected may sever from the part that believes they are lovable. These are not conscious decisions—they are survival instincts.

As adults, betrayal by those we trust—lovers, friends, family—can echo this early soul fracture. Losses, whether of people, dreams, or dignity, can trigger old wounds, causing further fragmentation. Repeated experiences of invalidation, overwork, or emotional disconnection from oneself or others may also cause subtle forms of soul dislocation.

Even in collective experiences—war, displacement, systemic oppression—the soul can splinter. When we feel unseen, unheard, or unloved, when we witness or participate in cruelty we cannot reconcile, when we are forced to silence our truth to be accepted, the soul bends. And if the pressure is too great, it breaks.

Soul Retrieval: The Call to Wholeness

Yet the soul is resilient. What was once sent away can be welcomed back. The practice of *soul retrieval* is the process of returning to ourselves—not by becoming someone new, but by remembering who we were before we began to forget.

Soul retrieval begins with listening. Stillness. A willingness to be present with what arises. This may take the form of meditation, journaling, therapy, time in nature, or simply conscious silence. You do not need grand rituals or elaborate ceremonies, though in some traditions, trained shamans or healers facilitate this process through deep spiritual journeying.

To retrieve the soul is to honour the wound without rushing its healing. It is not about fixing what is broken, but rather about sitting beside the brokenness with compassion until it softens into wholeness. Often, the parts of us that have gone quiet are not gone because they hate us—but because we stopped being safe for them. The body and soul crave environments of gentleness, honesty, and non-judgment. When we create those conditions within, the soul returns on its own.

You may recall a childhood memory, once too painful to touch, and now find yourself holding it with tenderness. You may feel emotions you've buried for years begin to rise—grief, anger, longing—and realize they are messengers, not enemies. You may dream of your younger self or see visions of yourself smiling in a forgotten moment. These are signs of the soul knocking.

Practices for Reclaiming the Lost Self

1. Speak to Yourself with Compassion:

Harshness drives the soul further away. The way we speak to ourselves must be the way we would speak to a hurt child—with patience, softness, and love. Soul retrieval cannot coexist with self-loathing. Each time you offer yourself gentleness, you build a bridge for the lost parts to return.

2. Revisit Old Wounds with New Eyes:

Sometimes, writing letters to your younger self—or visualizing a conversation with them—can allow the part of you that left to feel seen. Let them know that the world hurt them, but they are still worthy of love. Let them know they did nothing wrong.

3. Create Beauty Where Pain Once Lived:

Art, poetry, music, and dance are powerful tools. They bypass logic and speak directly to the soul. When you create from your pain, you give it voice—and in doing so, you welcome back what was silenced.

4. Embody the Self You Once Disowned:

Perhaps you stopped singing, drawing, playing, or speaking your truth. Reclaim those acts, however small. The soul loves embodiment. It thrives when we express, when we move, when we dare to be seen. Each courageous act is a signal: "You are safe to return."

5. Engage in Stillness and Sacred Listening:

Create space in your day for silence. Not to achieve something, but to simply be. The soul's voice is quiet. It does not shout. When the mind grows still, the soul begins to speak—not in words, but in feelings, images, insights.

The Gentle Nature of This Work

Soul retrieval is not an overnight transformation. It is not linear. You may find that pieces return and then retreat again. Some days you may feel illuminated with clarity, other days submerged in fog. This is part of the process. Healing unfolds in spirals, not straight lines.

Importantly, this work must be done gently. Force cannot retrieve the soul—only presence can. You cannot command your wholeness back with anger. You must invite it with love. Be patient with the timelines of your spirit. Trust that what left did so for a reason, and it will return when the conditions feel kind.

The Return of Aliveness

When the soul returns, life begins to feel different—though the outer world may look the same. Food tastes richer. Colours seem more vivid. Laughter arises more easily. You find yourself singing in the car for no reason. Tears come, not from despair, but from feeling. A kind of inner companionship blossoms.

You feel more *you*.

Decisions become easier because they arise from inner truth, not external pressure. You begin to recognize what aligns with your spirit and what does not. Toxic patterns fall away. You begin to choose relationships, work, and environments that nourish your integrity. You say no without guilt. You say yes with joy.

And most importantly, you remember that you were never truly broken—only fragmented. You were never lost—only hidden.

From Fragmentation to Integration

To retrieve the soul is not to deny what happened. It is not about pretending the trauma did not wound you. Rather, it is about Honouring your resilience while choosing not to live from the fracture anymore. You gather the lost pieces, hold them close, and welcome them home.

Integration is not perfection. It is not being happy all the time or finally having all the answers. It is knowing who you are, even when the world is uncertain. It is knowing your value, even when others cannot see it. It is being anchored in the deep knowing that within you is something whole, eternal, and unshakeable.

This is the gift of soul retrieval. Not just the return of a lost part—but the remembering of who you have always been.

TWENTY-SIX

PURPOSE — THE SOUL'S COMPASS

In the vast, unfolding journey of life, the question of purpose inevitably arises. It is a question whispered softly within the chambers of the soul — a question that seeks not an answer imposed from the outside, but an inner recognition of why we exist, what drives us, and how we might live in harmony with our deepest truths. To understand purpose as the soul's compass is to see it not as a rigid destination, but as a fluid and evolving guide, always pointing us toward alignment with our authentic selves and the meaning embedded in our experience.

The Soul's Longing and the Quest for Meaning

At the core of every human being is an ineffable longing — a pull toward something greater than mundane existence. This longing is not born out of mere desire or ambition, but from the soul's innate yearning for expression, connection, and fulfilment. The soul's compass is the internal sense that directs us toward this fulfilment, often through feelings, passions, and subtle nudges that transcend rational thought.

Purpose, then, is not simply a task to accomplish or a role to play. It is a deeper resonance with the essence of who we are, a tuning into the frequency of our own unique being. This compass guides us through life's complexities, uncertainties, and paradoxes, providing a north star that helps us navigate even the darkest nights of the soul.

Distinguishing Purpose from External Expectations

One of the great challenges in discovering and living our purpose lies in distinguishing it from external expectations and societal conditioning. From childhood, many of us absorb beliefs about success, worthiness, and "the right path" from parents, schools, culture, and media. These external narratives often shape what we think we should want or become, rather than what our soul truly seeks.

When purpose is confused with externally imposed goals, life can feel hollow, stressful, and unaligned. Even achievement can leave us feeling empty if it is not grounded in authentic passion and soul-led intention. Purpose, by contrast, arises from within and is often accompanied by a deep sense of peace, clarity, and joy—even amidst challenges.

Listening to the Soul's Language

The soul does not speak in words or logic alone. Its language is subtle — found in intuition, dreams, feelings of resonance or dissonance, moments of profound awe, and the quiet callings that stir the heart. Learning to listen to this language requires cultivating stillness and presence, creating inner space free from distraction.

Meditation, journaling, creative expression, and time spent in nature are powerful tools to attune ourselves to this inner voice. Through such practices, we begin to distinguish between the mind's chatter and the soul's whisper. The soul's guidance often feels like a gentle pull rather than a demand, a knowing rather than a conclusion.

Passion as a Beacon

Passion is often the first visible signpost on the path of purpose. When we engage with activities that stir our enthusiasm and ignite our curiosity, we touch the energy of the soul. These moments of passion are not accidental; they are clues left by the soul, illuminating the way toward deeper alignment.

However, passion alone is not purpose. Passion can be fleeting or superficial, whereas purpose encompasses a broader and more sustained commitment. The soul's compass encourages us to pursue passions that harmonize with our values and contribute meaningfully to our growth and the well-being of others.

Overcoming Resistance and Fear

Walking in alignment with our purpose often invites resistance. Fear of failure, rejection, or the unknown can obscure the soul's compass. Additionally, the comfort of familiar routines and the allure of external validation may keep us from venturing into uncharted territories.

Yet, these obstacles are not merely hindrances; they are integral to the journey. They offer opportunities for deepening courage, resilience, and self-trust. Each time we choose to follow our soul's guidance despite fear, we reclaim a part of our authentic power.

The Fluidity of Purpose

It is important to understand that purpose is not fixed or static. Life is a river in constant flow, and so is the expression of our purpose. As we grow, learn, and evolve, our soul's compass may shift direction, revealing new facets of our calling.

Embracing this fluidity frees us from rigid expectations and allows us to adapt gracefully to life's changes. It also invites a compassionate approach to self-discovery — recognizing that uncertainty is part of the process, not a failure.

Purpose Beyond the Self

While purpose is deeply personal, it is also inherently relational and communal. The soul's compass points not only toward self-realization but toward contribution and connection. When we align with our purpose, we naturally impact the world around us — through acts of kindness, creativity, leadership, or simply by being fully present.

This interconnectedness reveals that living our purpose is an act of service, weaving our individual threads into the broader fabric of humanity. It reminds us that our well-being and fulfilment are linked with that of others and the planet.

Practical Ways to Engage the Soul's Compass

Discovering and living your purpose is an ongoing practice. Here are some ways to nurture this relationship with your soul's compass:

1. **Create Daily Reflection Space:** Set aside moments each day for silence and introspection. Ask yourself open-ended questions like "What feels alive in me today?" or "Where is my energy drawn?"
2. **Tune into Emotions:** Notice which activities bring you joy, peace, or excitement, and which drain or frustrate you. Emotions are powerful indicators of alignment.
3. **Explore Curiosity:** Follow what genuinely interests you without judgment or pressure to produce results. Curiosity opens doors to new discoveries.
4. **Seek Support:** Engage with mentors, coaches, or communities that encourage authentic growth and exploration.
5. **Embrace Play and Creativity:** Often, the soul expresses itself through creative acts or playful engagement. Allow yourself freedom to experiment and express without expectation.
6. **Practice Compassion:** Be gentle with yourself in moments of doubt or confusion. Remember, purpose is a journey, not a checklist.

The Transformative Power of Purpose

Aligning with your soul's compass transforms not only how you experience life but also how you face suffering, loss, and uncertainty. Purpose provides a grounding force, a source of meaning that sustains through hardship.

When the soul's longing is acknowledged and embraced, life becomes a co-creation between the self and the larger mysteries of existence. It invites a deep trust that each step, whether clear or uncertain, is part of a meaningful unfolding.

Reflection

Ask yourself:

- What activities or moments make me feel most alive and connected?
- When have I felt the quiet voice of my soul guiding me?
- What fears or beliefs might be clouding my ability to follow my purpose?
- How can I cultivate daily practices to listen more closely to my inner compass?

The soul's compass is an invitation to live with depth, authenticity, and passion. It calls us to move beyond external expectations and rediscover the profound truth that our lives matter—not because of what we achieve, but because of who we are becoming.

By following this compass, we embrace a life that is not only personally fulfilling but also rich with the potential to inspire and uplift others. In this journey, purpose ceases to be a distant goal and becomes a living, breathing part of our every moment.

TWENTY-SEVEN
CREATING A SACRED INNER SPACE

In the tumultuous ebb and flow of daily life, the quest for inner peace is a profound and enduring journey. The sacred inner space is not a place on any map but a refuge we cultivate within ourselves — a sanctuary where silence, stillness, and presence dwell. It is a place where the soul finds respite, the mind gains clarity, and the heart opens freely. To create this sacred inner space is to establish a sanctuary that holds and nurtures the fullness of our being.

This chapter invites you to embark on the delicate art of crafting such a space — through journaling, reflection, and sacred routines. These practices are not mere tasks or rituals, but gateways that help us step out of the noise of external demands and into the gentle embrace of our own true nature.

The Inner Space: What Does It Mean?

Imagine a quiet garden within your consciousness, a clearing in the dense forest of thought and distraction. This is the sacred inner space — a place that is always accessible, yet often overlooked. It exists beyond fleeting emotions and surface identities, deeper than worries or aspirations.

Creating this space means intentionally slowing down to honour yourself, cultivating presence with your own thoughts, feelings, and sensations. It is not an escape from reality, but a conscious engagement with it from a place of centeredness.

The sacred inner space invites us to meet ourselves with kindness, curiosity, and respect. Here, the boundaries between body, mind, and soul soften, revealing the wholeness that is our essence.

Why Create a Sacred Inner Space?

The modern world relentlessly pulls us outward — to obligations, screens, noise, and relentless busyness. This constant external pull fractures our attention and fragments our sense of self. Without inner sanctuary, we risk losing connection with our deeper wisdom, values, and authentic desires.

A sacred inner space acts as an anchor amid chaos. It is a place where you can:

- **Receive clarity:** When overwhelmed, the inner space clarifies what matters most.
- **Heal wounds:** Emotional pain and tension soften in the presence of self-compassion.
- **Gain perspective:** Stepping back from reactive impulses allows wiser responses.
- **Connect with the soul:** The inner sanctuary reveals your soul's whispers and longings.
- **Restore balance:** Physical, emotional, and mental harmony arise from regular tending to this space.

In essence, it is a sacred dialogue between your external life and your inner truth.

Journaling: Writing as a Sacred Dialogue

Journaling is a profound tool for creating and entering the sacred inner space. It is a form of conversation with yourself — a place where the mind's clutter can be untangled and the soul's voice can be heard clearly.

Beyond the Surface

The power of journaling lies not in neat sentences or grammatical perfection but in honesty and openness. It invites you to write without censoring, to explore thoughts and emotions freely, and to witness your own inner world without judgment.

Through journaling, you may discover:

- Patterns in your thinking or behaviour that were previously hidden.
- Unexpressed feelings waiting for acknowledgment.
- Inner conflicts that seek resolution.
- Insights that point toward your deeper purpose.

Sacred Journaling Practices

- **Set intention:** Before beginning, breathe deeply and affirm that this time is sacred, dedicated to self-discovery.
- **Use prompts mindfully:** Questions like "What am I feeling right now?" or "What does my soul need to hear today?" can open new avenues.
- **Write without expectation:** Allow your pen to flow freely, even if the words seem disjointed or unclear. The act itself is transformative.
- **Revisit with compassion:** Occasionally, return to previous entries not to judge but to witness growth and change.

Journaling is less about producing a polished product and more about creating a container for your inner landscape to unfold.

Reflection: The Art of Deep Listening

Reflection complements journaling by cultivating a posture of deep listening — to yourself, to your experiences, and to the silent wisdom within. Reflection requires slowing down and creating mental space to process life's unfolding.

Reflection as a Sacred Pause

In the sacred inner space, reflection becomes a pause — a moment to breathe between actions, to step back and observe with openness. It asks, "What have I learned from this moment? What is calling for my attention beneath the surface?"

Reflection transforms everyday moments into opportunities for insight and growth. It moves us beyond reactive living into conscious presence.

Cultivating Reflective Practices

- **Daily Pause:** Take a few minutes at the end of each day to quietly review your experiences, emotions, and reactions.
- **Mindful Inquiry:** Ask yourself gentle questions such as "What brought me joy today?" or "Where did I feel disconnected?"
- **Presence in Nature:** Spend time outdoors, letting the natural world reflect your inner state and inspire contemplation.
- **Guided Meditation:** Use meditative practices that focus on observing thoughts without attachment, deepening your capacity to listen inwardly.

Reflection is not about finding immediate answers but about cultivating trust in the unfolding process of self-awareness.

Sacred Routines: Creating Rituals to Anchor the Inner Space

Routines imbued with intention and reverence become rituals — sacred acts that honour your inner sanctuary. Sacred routines offer consistency and structure, helping to anchor you in presence and peace amid the unpredictability of life.

Why Rituals Matter

Rituals create rhythm and meaning, transforming ordinary actions into acts of self-care and spiritual connection. They mark time as sacred and provide a framework within which the soul can breathe.

Through ritual, the sacred inner space becomes an active part of your daily existence, not a rare or distant ideal.

Examples of Sacred Routines

- **Morning Grounding:** Begin your day with simple breathwork, a gratitude practice, or gentle stretching to awaken your body and mind in harmony.

- **Evening Unwinding:** Establish a ritual to close the day — lighting a candle, reading a poem, or writing in your journal — signalling transition to rest.
- **Movement as Meditation:** Engage in mindful movement such as yoga, tai chi, or walking meditation that connects body and breath with presence.
- **Sacred Space Creation:** Dedicate a corner of your home for objects that inspire calm and reverence — crystals, plants, meaningful symbols — inviting you to pause and reflect.
- **Rituals of Nourishment:** Approach eating as a sacred act, savouring each bite with mindfulness and gratitude, deepening your connection to your body.

Each ritual need not be elaborate; simplicity and heartfelt intention are what make them sacred.

The Role of Boundaries in Sacred Space

Creating sacred inner space also involves setting healthy boundaries with external demands and distractions. Saying "no" to what drains your energy and "yes" to what nourishes your soul is a radical act of self-love.

Boundaries protect the sanctity of your inner space, allowing you to guard your time, energy, and attention. This can mean limiting screen time, creating quiet hours, or consciously choosing who and what you engage with.

Honouring boundaries is a declaration that your inner sanctuary matters — that your presence with yourself is not negotiable.

Challenges and Patience on the Path

Building and maintaining a sacred inner space is a tender process, often met with challenges. The mind resists silence; distractions abound; life's demands pull us outward. Sometimes, our efforts feel futile or superficial.

Yet, the very persistence in returning to this space, again and again, cultivates resilience and depth. Each moment spent in quiet presence, each word written in vulnerability, each ritual performed with intention strengthens your connection with yourself.

Patience is essential. The sacred inner space is not a prize to win but a relationship to nurture.

The Fruits of Sacred Inner Space

When we create and tend this sacred inner space, profound transformation unfolds:

- **Emotional Balance:** We become less reactive, more grounded, and able to respond with clarity.
- **Enhanced Creativity:** The mind's chatter quiets, allowing inspiration and insight to surface.
- **Deeper Self-Knowledge:** We develop a nuanced understanding of our desires, fears, and patterns.
- **Spiritual Connection:** The soul's voice becomes clearer, guiding us with wisdom beyond intellect.
- **Peace Amidst Chaos:** We carry a sanctuary within, untouched by external storms.

Ultimately, the sacred inner space is a wellspring of love and acceptance — the place where we meet ourselves fully and find the courage to live authentically.

Reflection and Practice

Take time this week to begin or deepen your sacred inner space practice. Here are some prompts and exercises to guide you:

1. **Journaling Prompt:**
   "What does a sacred inner space look and feel like to me? What do I need to create that space within myself?"
2. **Reflection Exercise:**
   Set a timer for five minutes. Sit quietly and breathe deeply. Notice any thoughts or sensations without judgment. Allow yourself to simply be present.
3. **Ritual Creation:**
   Choose one simple action to transform into a daily ritual — lighting a candle, sipping tea mindfully, or stretching. Approach

it with intention and presence.

4. **Boundary Check:**
   Reflect on where you might need to set firmer boundaries to
   protect your inner peace. What small step can you take today to
   honour your sacred space?

Creating a sacred inner space is a profound act of self-respect
and soul care. It is the foundation upon which all other growth,
healing, and purpose rest. When you commit to this inner
sanctuary, you gift yourself the possibility of living fully — deeply
connected, authentically present, and aligned with the soul's
deepest wisdom.

May this chapter be an invitation and a companion on your
journey inward — toward the sacred garden that blooms quietly,
always within reach.

TWENTY-EIGHT
THE SOUL'S HUNGER FOR TRUTH

In the quiet moments before dawn, when the world still slumbers under the veil of night, there is a profound stirring within us—a subtle, yet relentless yearning. It is the soul's hunger for truth. This hunger is ancient and unyielding, a call that echoes through the chambers of our being, inviting us to awaken to what is real, authentic, and whole. To live in truth is to live in alignment with the essence of who we are; to deny truth is to invite suffering, fragmentation, and inner discord.

This chapter unfolds the intricate relationship between truth and the soul, revealing how denial starves us and how the courageous act of truth-telling becomes nourishment that restores vitality, clarity, and peace.

The Nature of the Soul's Hunger

What is this hunger? It is not a mere desire for factual accuracy or external verification, but a profound craving for existential authenticity. The soul longs to be seen and known—not just by others, but by ourselves. It seeks coherence between our inner experience and outer expression.

This hunger is like a primal thirst. When unquenched, it leads to a deep malaise—a restlessness that no distraction or pleasure can assuage. It manifests as a feeling that something is "off," an unnameable dissatisfaction, a sense of disconnection from the self and the world.

Philosophers, mystics, and poets across ages have recognized this hunger. To live fully, they say, we must face the truth of our existence, however uncomfortable or painful.

Living in Denial: The Soul's Starvation

Denial is a defense mechanism, a shield we raise to protect ourselves from truths too overwhelming or threatening. We may deny our emotions, the realities of our relationships, or the deeper calls of our spirit. While denial offers temporary refuge, it is ultimately a form of self-betrayal.

When we live in denial, the soul suffers in silence. It is akin to a garden starved of sunlight—though the soil remains fertile, the seeds of growth cannot sprout without the nourishing light of truth.

Denial fractures the self. It creates dissonance between what we know deep down and what we allow ourselves to admit. This dissonance generates inner conflict, confusion, and a persistent sense of inauthenticity.

Psychologically, denial may protect us from pain, but existentially, it deprives the soul of its essential sustenance—recognition, acceptance, and integration.

The Many Faces of Denial

Denial is not always blatant or conscious. It wears many masks:

- **Minimization:** Downplaying feelings or events to avoid discomfort.
- **Projection:** Attributing our own unwanted truths to others.
- **Rationalization:** Creating justifications to avoid facing harsh realities.
- **Avoidance:** Distracting ourselves with busyness or numbing substances.
- **Silencing:** Refusing to speak or acknowledge truths within ourselves.

Each form of denial distances us from our soul's true voice, muffling the call to authenticity.

The Courage to Face Truth

Truth-telling—first to ourselves and then to the world—requires profound courage. It demands vulnerability, humility, and a willingness to be seen without masks or pretenses.

Yet, this courage is the gateway to freedom. As the philosopher Soren Kierkegaard wrote, "The truth is the highest thing a man may keep." To keep truth is to honour our dignity and wholeness.

Facing truth is not a one-time event but an ongoing practice. It means waking up daily to what is true in our heart, even when it contradicts societal expectations, personal fears, or comforting illusions.

Truth as Nourishment for the Soul

When we embrace truth, the soul receives what it has longed for—clarity, integrity, and alignment. Truth lights the path out of confusion and self-deception.

Nourishing the soul through truth:

- **Restores wholeness:** Integrates fragmented parts of the self into a coherent identity.
- **Heals wounds:** Allows buried pain to surface and transform through acknowledgment.
- **Frees energy:** Releases the psychic weight of hiding and pretending.
- **Builds trust:** Strengthens the relationship with oneself and others through honesty.
- **Deepens connection:** Opens the heart to authentic relationships and spiritual insight.

Truth is not always comfortable, but it is always liberating.

The Paradox of Truth and Compassion

Honesty does not mean harshness. The soul's hunger for truth thrives best in an environment of compassion—both for ourselves and others.

We must learn to speak truths gently and receive them with tenderness. Self-compassion allows us to hold painful realities without judgment or despair.

In this light, truth-telling becomes a sacred act of kindness—a healing balm that softens suffering rather than intensifying it.

Practices to Nourish the Soul's Hunger for Truth

1. Radical Self-Honesty

Begin with an unwavering commitment to be truthful with yourself. This means:

- Observing thoughts and feelings without censorship.
- Naming emotions honestly, even when they feel uncomfortable.
- Questioning assumptions and beliefs with curiosity rather than defense.

Radical self-honesty creates a fertile ground where truth can grow.

2. Journaling as Witness

Writing becomes a sacred dialogue with the self, where hidden truths can emerge from the shadows. Approach journaling as a compassionate witness, not a judge.

Use prompts like:

- *What am I avoiding?*
- *What truths have I been afraid to face?*
- *What does my soul need to know right now?*

3. Mindful Reflection

Set aside moments to pause and observe your internal state. Mindfulness helps uncover truths beneath reactive thoughts and habitual denial.

4. Truthful Communication

Practice speaking your truth with kindness and clarity to trusted others. Begin with small truths and build toward greater openness.

5. Embracing Vulnerability

Recognize that vulnerability is the gateway to truth. When you allow yourself to be seen fully, your soul breathes freely.

The Soul's Hunger and the Collective Dimension

Our individual hunger for truth is mirrored in the collective consciousness. Societies built on denial—whether of injustice, ecological crises, or social inequities—suffer deeply.

Healing the soul's hunger for truth is not only personal but profoundly political and ecological. When we reclaim truth in ourselves, we contribute to a larger movement of awakening and healing.

Truth-telling becomes an act of courage that ripples outward, challenging illusions and inspiring authenticity in others.

The Transformative Power of Truth

Truth has the power to transform suffering into wisdom, fragmentation into wholeness, and isolation into belonging. The soul's hunger for truth is an invitation to a deeper life—a life lived not in fear or denial, but in radiant awareness.

By feeding this hunger, we reclaim our sovereignty and step into our fullest potential. We become alchemists of the soul, turning the lead of illusion into the gold of clarity.

Closing Reflection

Take a moment now to listen to your own soul's hunger. What truths is it calling you to face? What parts of yourself long to be seen and acknowledged?

Remember, truth is not a destination but a path—a lifelong journey of discovery, courage, and grace.

May you meet your soul's hunger with open eyes and an open heart. May truth be the sustenance that nourishes your deepest self and guides you home.

TWENTY-NINE
SOUL LOVE VS. EGO LOVE

Love—perhaps the most spoken of and yet least understood of human experiences—dwells at the heart of our being. Yet, the forms love takes are as varied and complex as the human soul itself. We often mistake the surface reflections of love—those fleeting, self-centred attractions and attachments—for its deepest essence. This chapter invites us to peel back the layers of illusion to discern the difference between ego love and soul love: between love that nourishes the self and love that awakens the soul.

The Many Faces of Love: A Mirror to the Self

Love, in its broadest sense, is a mirror. It reflects back to us who we are—our hopes, our wounds, our shadows, and our light. But the reflection depends on the lens through which we view it. Is it the lens of the ego, tinted with fear and desire? Or the lens of the soul, transparent and vast?

Ego love is conditional, transactional, and often rooted in scarcity. It seeks validation, possession, or safety. It is driven by the need to fill emptiness or to prove worthiness. This love can look like infatuation, obsession, co-dependency, or control, and is often marked by anxiety, jealousy, or fear of loss.

Soul love, by contrast, is unconditional, generous, and rooted in abundance. It emerges from the awareness of shared existence, interconnectedness, and the sacredness of being. Soul love accepts imperfection, embraces vulnerability, and seeks not to possess but to liberate.

Ego Love: The Love of Separation

The ego is the part of us that identifies with labels, roles, and the constructed self-image. Ego love mirrors this identification by clinging to surface qualities—appearance, status, achievements, or idealized notions of "the other." It loves what it perceives as separate from itself, often leading to attachment born of fear rather than freedom born of trust.

In ego love:

- **Attachment governs:** We fear losing the beloved because our sense of self feels threatened.
- **Comparison arises:** We measure ourselves and others, fuelling competition rather than compassion.
- **Possession is sought:** Love becomes a contract of ownership, where freedom is sacrificed for security.
- **Conditional acceptance reigns:** Love is given only when certain conditions are met—beauty, success, conformity.

This love is like a flame fuelled by oil—bright but volatile, needing constant attention lest it flicker and die.

Soul Love: The Love of Unity

Soul love flows from a different wellspring. It arises when we recognize that the beloved is not separate but an extension of our own being. In soul love:

- **Freedom is honoured:** Both selves are free to grow, change, and express without fear of abandonment.
- **Vulnerability is embraced:** Authenticity is shared without masks or defenses.
- **Acceptance is unconditional:** Love holds space for flaws, wounds, and transformations.

- **Presence is given:** Love is found in deep listening, shared silence, and profound connection beyond words.

This love is like an endless ocean—vast, deep, and sustaining, inviting surrender rather than grasping.

How Ego Love Begins and Ends

Ego love often begins with infatuation—a dazzling mirage that captivates the senses and inflates the self. The ego delights in being desired, admired, and confirmed. It may appear as passion, urgency, or obsession.

Yet, ego love carries the seeds of its own demise. When the initial illusion fades, the fragile foundation of attachment and control often crumbles. Conflicts arise, trust erodes, and fear infiltrates.

The ego's need to protect itself can transform love into a battlefield—where blame, resentment, and withdrawal replace warmth and trust.

How Soul Love Emerges and Endures

Soul love emerges from the courage to face oneself and the beloved honestly. It is nurtured by patience, forgiveness, and the willingness to be imperfect.

Soul love is not dependent on external conditions. It is a practice—a commitment to presence, compassion, and growth together.

This love endures because it is not an attachment but a meeting of essences. It invites each person to fully inhabit their individuality while recognizing the unity beneath.

The Dance Between Ego and Soul in Love

No human love is purely ego or purely soul. Rather, love is a dynamic dance where ego and soul intertwine.

At times, the ego may seize the reins—leading to jealousy, fear, or control. At other moments, the soul's voice calls for surrender, trust, and boundless compassion.

The challenge—and the gift—is to cultivate awareness so that ego impulses are recognized and held lightly, while soul impulses are nurtured and expanded.

Recognizing Ego Love in Your Relationships

To discern the quality of love in your relationships, look for signs of ego love:

- Do you feel anxious about losing the other or controlling their choices?
- Is your love tied to specific conditions or expectations?
- Do conflicts escalate into power struggles or withdrawal?
- Do you find yourself comparing your relationship to others or idealizing perfection?
- Does love feel like a performance or a contract?

If these patterns dominate, it may be time to gently examine how ego love operates in your life.

Cultivating Soul Love Within Yourself

Before soul love can be fully expressed outwardly, it must be cultivated within. The soul's love first awakens in the relationship with yourself.

Begin by:

- Embracing your imperfections with kindness and acceptance.
- Listening deeply to your own needs, desires, and boundaries.
- Practicing self-compassion when fear or judgment arise.
- Exploring your wounds with curiosity and healing intent.
- Nurturing your passions and soul-longings without apology.

When you love yourself with the depth of the soul, you create the fertile soil from which authentic love with others can grow.

Soul Love as Transformation

Soul love transforms not only the lovers but also the very nature of love itself. It turns love from a possession into a gift, from a source of fear into a source of freedom.

This transformation happens through:

- **Presence:** Loving fully in the present moment, without clinging to past grievances or future fears.
- **Honesty:** Speaking truth with gentleness and listening with an open heart.
- **Generosity:** Offering love without expectation of return or control.
- **Healing:** Supporting each other's growth, even when it involves pain or separation.
- **Spiritual Awareness:** Recognizing the sacredness in the beloved as a reflection of the divine.

The Role of Vulnerability in Soul Love

Vulnerability is the language of soul love. It demands courage—to be seen, to reveal wounds, and to risk rejection.

Yet vulnerability also births intimacy—the deep, unshakable connection that transcends appearances and circumstances.

In soul love, vulnerability is not weakness but strength. It is the bridge from isolation to union.

Soul Love Beyond Romance

While often associated with romantic relationships, soul love extends far beyond. It animates friendships, family bonds, and even our relationship with life itself.

Soul love is the force that fosters forgiveness, understanding, and unconditional support in all forms of connection.

It is the current running through compassionate action, creative expression, and spiritual devotion.

Challenges on the Path to Soul Love

The path to soul love is not without obstacles. The ego resists surrender, preferring the illusion of control.

Fear of abandonment, betrayal, or inadequacy can cause retreat into ego defenses.

Old wounds may trigger patterns of mistrust and avoidance.

Yet, each challenge is also an invitation to deepen the practice—to meet fear with presence, to heal wounds with compassion, and to choose love over separation.

Practical Steps Toward Soul Love

1. **Self-Inquiry:** Regularly question your motives in love. Are you seeking to possess or to free? To fix or to accept?
2. **Mindful Presence:** Practice being fully present with yourself and others without judgment or distraction.
3. **Open Communication:** Foster honest and compassionate dialogue about feelings, needs, and boundaries.
4. **Embrace Impermanence:** Accept that all relationships evolve and that holding too tightly causes suffering.
5. **Celebrate Individuality:** Encourage growth and freedom in yourself and your loved ones.
6. **Practice Forgiveness:** Release resentment and grudges to open space for healing.
7. **Cultivate Gratitude:** Appreciate the gifts of connection, even amidst challenges.

Conclusion: The Soul's Call to Love Deeply

In the end, love is the language of the soul—a sacred dialogue that calls us beyond the self-imposed limits of ego.

It is an invitation to awaken to a deeper reality where love is not scarcity but abundance, not possession but freedom, not fear but courage.

To answer this call is to embark on the most profound journey of all—the journey home to ourselves and each other, where soul love dwells eternally.

THIRTY

BEFRIEND YOUR SOUL, HEAL YOUR LIFE

To befriend your soul is to step into a relationship unlike any other—the most enduring, honest, and transformative friendship you will ever know. Your soul is not a distant, ethereal concept reserved for mystics or poets. It is the living essence of who you are, the inner companion who has walked with you through every joy and sorrow, every triumph and failure. It is the friend who asks nothing but your presence and offers everything: wisdom, healing, and unconditional love.

This chapter unfolds as an invitation and a guide—a call to cultivate this sacred friendship and, in doing so, to heal your life from the inside out.

The Oldest Friend Within

Consider the soul as the oldest friend you have ever had. From the moment of your first breath, this friend has been there, silently witnessing your unfolding story. Unlike external friendships, which may waver or falter, your soul's friendship is unshakable because it is rooted not in circumstance but in being.

Yet, how often do we forget this friend? How often do we neglect the quiet presence that yearns for attention, understanding, and trust? In the busyness and noise of life, the soul's voice is easy to overlook, mistaken for silence or absence.

To befriend your soul is to remember, to turn inward, and to recognize that this friend has never left your side. It is to welcome yourself fully, without judgment or condition.

Why Befriend Your Soul?

The act of befriending your soul is not merely poetic; it has profound practical consequences for your well-being. When you honour your soul as a trusted friend:

- **You cultivate self-compassion:** You learn to treat yourself with the kindness and patience you would offer a beloved companion.
- **You gain clarity:** The soul's wisdom guides you beyond fleeting desires and fears, illuminating your true path.
- **You foster resilience:** In the face of life's inevitable challenges, your soul's steady presence provides strength and grounding.
- **You experience wholeness:** Healing the relationship with your soul restores a sense of integration and peace within.
- **You deepen connection:** With your soul as friend, your relationships with others gain authenticity and depth.

In essence, befriending your soul is the foundation for a healed, vibrant life.

The Barriers to Friendship

Before friendship can flourish, it is essential to recognize the barriers that often stand between us and our soul:

1. Fear and Distrust

Past wounds—betrayal, rejection, trauma—can make us wary of opening to our own inner self. The soul may seem like an unknown, even threatening territory.

2. Distraction and Busyness

Modern life pulls attention outward with endless stimuli. The soul's subtle voice can easily be drowned in noise and haste.

3. Self-Judgment and Shame

We often view parts of ourselves with harshness, rejecting aspects that feel vulnerable or unworthy. This alienates us from our soul's unconditional embrace.

4. Ego's Resistance

The ego thrives on control, certainty, and separation. It may resist the surrender and openness that befriending the soul requires.

Steps Toward Friendship

Just as any friendship takes time, care, and patience, so does the friendship with your soul. Here are some guiding principles to nurture this bond:

1. Show Up Regularly

Friendship requires presence. Set aside moments daily—however brief—to turn inward. This could be through meditation, journaling, or simply sitting in quiet awareness.

The soul does not demand grand gestures. It thrives on consistent, genuine attention.

2. Practice Compassionate Listening

When you listen to your soul, do so without interruption or judgment. Allow thoughts, feelings, images, or sensations to arise and pass like clouds across a sky.

Resist the urge to analyse or fix. Instead, offer acceptance and curiosity.

3. Honour Your Feelings

The soul speaks often through emotion. Rather than suppress or deny feelings, embrace them as messengers. Joy, sorrow, fear, and hope alike carry the soul's language.

In befriending your soul, feelings become sacred conversations rather than obstacles.

4. Create Rituals of Connection

Rituals honour the sacredness of friendship. These might include lighting a candle, writing letters to your soul, or creating a special space for reflection.

Rituals anchor your intention and deepen the sense of reverence.

5. Invite Creativity

Soul friendship blossoms in creative expression. Painting, music, dance, poetry, or movement can open channels to your deepest self.

Creative acts become dialogues, where the soul's wisdom emerges naturally.

6. Seek Stillness and Solitude

In silence and solitude, the soul's voice can be heard clearly. Embrace moments of being alone not as loneliness but as opportunities to commune with your inner friend.

Healing Through Friendship

Befriending your soul is also an act of healing—repairing the fractures caused by life's hardships.

Healing Old Wounds

When life wounds run deep, the soul carries the imprint. But the friendship offers a safe space where these wounds can be gently acknowledged and tenderly cared for.

The soul does not rush or demand. It waits patiently for the courage to face pain, encouraging forgiveness and release.

Reclaiming Lost Parts

Sometimes, trauma or neglect causes parts of our soul to withdraw or fragment. Friendship invites these lost parts home, restoring wholeness.

Through compassionate presence, we invite our fractured selves to reintegrate, healing the wounds of separation.

Transforming Self-Criticism

The voice of harsh self-judgment can be silenced by the soft, steady voice of the soul as friend. Where the ego condemns, the soul consoles; where doubt reigns, the soul encourages.

The Dance of Friendship and Growth

Friendship with the soul is not static; it is a living, evolving dance. As you grow and change, so does your relationship with this inner companion.

There will be moments of closeness and moments of distance. Times when the soul's voice is loud and clear, and times when it feels muffled or hidden.

Trust this rhythm. Trust that your soul's friendship is resilient, capable of withstanding all seasons.

The Soul's Wisdom for Life

Through friendship, your soul becomes a guide, offering profound insights:

- **Authenticity:** Your soul encourages you to live truthfully, shedding masks and false roles.
- **Purpose:** It whispers your unique calling and gifts, urging you to express your essence.
- **Boundaries:** Your soul teaches the importance of saying "no" to what drains you and "yes" to what nourishes you.
- **Gratitude:** It reminds you to appreciate the small miracles woven into each day.
- **Compassion:** Your soul's love extends beyond yourself, fostering kindness toward all beings.

Friendship as a Practice of Presence

Ultimately, befriending your soul is a practice of presence—being fully here, now, with yourself.

It is the antidote to alienation, fragmentation, and despair.

Presence in friendship with your soul awakens a deep trust: that no matter what life brings, you are never truly alone.

A Loving Invitation

So here is the invitation, simple yet profound: turn inward with kindness. Meet your soul as you would an old friend—without expectations, without judgment, with open arms and an open heart.

In this friendship, discover not only yourself but the healing of your life—the unfolding of your true nature, radiant and whole.

Reflection Exercise: Writing to Your Soul

Take a moment to write a letter to your soul. Begin with words of greeting and gratitude. Share your fears, hopes, or questions. Write freely, as if to a cherished friend. Then, listen silently for any response, trusting that the soul communicates beyond words.

Closing Thoughts

The journey of befriending your soul is lifelong and ever-renewing. It asks only for your willingness to show up, to listen, and to love.

In the sacred friendship between you and your soul lies the power to heal, to grow, and to live with profound joy and peace.

May you walk this path gently, courageously, and with open heart.

THIRTY-ONE
THE INNER TEAM

Walking in Harmony with Body and Soul

In the vast and intricate theatre of our existence, three distinct players share the stage, each vital, each unique: the mind, the body, and the soul. Too often, we regard these as separate, even conflicting, forces within us — the mind commanding, the body resisting, the soul whispering from a distance. But what if they were not adversaries? What if, instead, they were members of an inner team, each with a role to play, each deserving respect and collaboration?

This chapter is an exploration of that sacred alliance: how to live in balance by inviting the mind, body, and soul to work not in opposition but in concert — a harmonious inner team.

The Three Pillars Within

To understand the concept of the inner team, we must first appreciate the nature and gifts of each member.

The Mind: The Analyst and Planner

The mind is the seat of thought, logic, memory, and decision-making. It is the architect of plans, the solver of problems, and the decipherer of experience. The mind gives us clarity and structure, enabling us to navigate the complexities of life with reason.

Yet, the mind can also be restless, critical, and anxious, caught in loops of worry or doubt. When it dominates unchecked, it may fragment our experience, disconnecting us from the fullness of being.

The Body: The Vessel and Sensor

The body is our living presence in the world. It breathes, moves, feels, and senses. It is the instrument through which we experience touch, pleasure, pain, and vitality. The body anchors us to the present moment and offers invaluable wisdom through sensations and intuition.

However, the body can feel burdensome when ignored, uncomfortable when disrespected, or rebellious when harmed. When we neglect its needs or dismiss its messages, the body may express distress through illness or discomfort.

The Soul: The Essence and Guide

The soul is the essence of our being — the spark of life that carries meaning, purpose, and connection to something greater. It is the voice of deep knowing, love, and spiritual longing. The soul urges us toward authenticity, growth, and transcendence.

Yet the soul is subtle and easily drowned out by the noise of daily life or the chatter of the mind. When ignored, the soul's voice may fade into silence or manifest as a sense of emptiness or disconnection.

When the Team Falls Apart

Most of us have experienced moments when the inner team fractures:

- The mind criticizes the body for its limitations, demanding perfection.
- The body rebels through fatigue or pain when the soul's yearnings are ignored.
- The soul feels unheard, overshadowed by the mind's endless analysis or the body's urgent needs.

This internal discord breeds tension, confusion, and imbalance, manifesting externally as stress, anxiety, or a lack of fulfilment.

To heal this fragmentation, we must learn to foster cooperation among the mind, body, and soul — recognizing that each has wisdom and value.

Cultivating Inner Cooperation

1. Acknowledging Each Member's Role

The first step toward harmony is acknowledgment. Each part of you deserves recognition:

- Thank the mind for its ability to think, plan, and learn.
- Honour the body for its strength, resilience, and sensations.
- Respect the soul for its depth, intuition, and longing.

By affirming each, you create an atmosphere of respect and openness.

2. Listening Without Judgment

Practice listening inwardly to each voice without judgment or preference. When a sensation arises, notice it without labelling it good or bad. When a thought emerges, observe it without immediately accepting or rejecting it. When a soulful urge beckons, honour its presence without skepticism.

This neutral, compassionate listening invites dialogue among the inner team.

3. Facilitating Dialogue

Imagine the mind, body, and soul as members of a council. When making a decision, invite each to speak and share their perspective. The mind might offer practical concerns, the body might reveal physical sensations or energy levels, and the soul might express values or deeper purpose.

Through this inner dialogue, decisions become more balanced and integrated.

Practices to Strengthen the Inner Team

Mindfulness and Presence

Mindfulness practice allows us to observe thoughts, bodily sensations, and emotions with gentle awareness. This practice dissolves barriers between mind and body and opens the door to the soul's quiet voice.

Body Awareness and Movement

Regularly tuning into your body through yoga, dance, or simply noticing breath and posture nurtures the body's wisdom and signals. When the body feels seen and cared for, it becomes a willing partner in the inner team.

Soul Connection through Reflection

Journaling, meditation, prayer, or time in nature can cultivate the soul's voice. These sacred spaces allow us to explore our deepest desires, fears, and truths, reconnecting with our essence.

The Power of Balance

When the inner team works together, the result is profound:

- **Clarity** emerges from the mind's analysis, tempered by the body's intuition and the soul's insight.
- **Energy** flows freely as the body is nurtured, the mind focused, and the soul inspired.
- **Resilience** is strengthened by the soul's steadiness, the mind's adaptability, and the body's strength.
- **Joy** becomes fuller as pleasures are felt in the body, understood by the mind, and embraced by the soul.

Balance does not mean perfection or absence of conflict. Rather, it is the willingness to hold differences with compassion, curiosity, and respect.

Wisdom from the Inner Team

The inner team teaches us a larger truth: that our well-being depends on integration — not separation.

It is a reminder that life's challenges are best met not by a single faculty alone but by the collective wisdom of our whole being.

As you move forward, practice inviting your mind, body, and soul into conversations about your choices, your dreams, and your healing. Ask:

- What does my mind see clearly here?
- What sensations or signals is my body offering?
- What does my soul long for?

Closing Reflection

The inner team is your lifelong companion, a source of strength, wisdom, and love.

When you embrace this partnership, you transform your relationship with yourself and the world. You live not fragmented or at war within, but in harmony — fully alive, fully present, fully whole.

May you nurture this sacred team with patience and joy.

THIRTY-TWO

SETTING BOUNDARIES WITH LOVE

In the dance of life, the ability to set boundaries is an essential rhythm—one that ensures balance, respect, and nourishment for our entire being. Boundaries are not walls built in fear or defense, but sacred lines drawn with tenderness, clarity, and love. They mark the spaces where our body and soul say, "Here is where I begin, and here is where I end."

This chapter explores the profound wisdom of Honouring limits—not as restrictions or punishments, but as acts of respect and compassion toward ourselves. To set boundaries is to listen deeply to the needs of our body and soul and to answer with care and courage.

The Gift and Misunderstanding of Boundaries

Boundaries often carry a misunderstood weight. In a culture that prizes endless productivity, pleasing others, and pushing past discomfort, boundaries can be seen as selfish or weak. But this misunderstanding arises from confusion about what boundaries truly are.

Boundaries are not barriers to connection, but invitations to authentic relationship—with ourselves and others. They protect the sacredness of our body's health and our soul's peace. Without boundaries, we risk losing ourselves in exhaustion, resentment, or fragmentation.

Why Boundaries Matter

For the Body: The Language of Limits

Our body speaks to us constantly, offering signals about its well-being through sensations of fatigue, pain, or ease. When we honour these signals by setting limits—choosing rest over relentless work, saying no to excessive demands, nourishing ourselves with what feels good—we affirm the body's inherent wisdom.

Ignoring these signals, pushing beyond what feels sustainable, or dismissing discomfort as weakness is a form of disrespect. The body's boundaries are not obstacles; they are life-affirming guides.

For the Soul: Guarding Sacred Space

The soul, delicate and profound, requires space for reflection, growth, and healing. It thrives in moments of silence, solitude, and self-honesty. When we fail to protect this inner sanctuary by overcommitting or surrendering to external pressures, the soul grows tired, fragmented, and lost.

Setting boundaries with love means saying no to what drains the soul and yes to what nourishes its light. It is an act of guarding the sacred fire within.

Recognizing Your Boundaries

To set boundaries with love, you must first know your limits. This is a practice of self-awareness and gentle inquiry.

Tune Into Physical Signals

Notice when your body feels tense, tired, or overwhelmed. These are early messages signalling the need for pause or adjustment.

Ask yourself:

- When do I feel most alive and free in my body?
- When do I feel drained or uncomfortable?
- What physical sensations arise when I say "yes" too much?

Observe Emotional Responses

Emotions often accompany boundary signals. Feelings of irritation, resentment, or anxiety can be clues that your limits are being crossed.

Ask yourself:

- What emotions arise when I feel overextended?
- When have I felt guilty or fearful about saying no?
- How do I feel when I honour my limits?

Listen to the Soul's Whisper

The soul's guidance is subtle but persistent. It may manifest as a longing for rest, a craving for solitude, or a yearning to protect your energy.

Ask yourself:

- What does my soul need to feel safe and nourished?
- What activities or relationships leave me feeling expanded or diminished?
- How can I create sacred space for my soul daily?

Boundaries as Acts of Love

Setting boundaries is often portrayed as a defensive move—an act of "putting up walls." But reframing boundaries as acts of love transforms them into gifts—to yourself and others.

Love for Your Body

When you say "no" to overwork, unhealthy habits, or harmful environments, you are telling your body: "I see you. I hear you. I will protect you."

This loving attention honours the body's needs for rest, movement, nutrition, and healing. Boundaries become invitations to treat the body as the sacred vessel it is.

Love for Your Soul

When you create time for reflection, decline invitations that drain your spirit, or choose relationships that uplift you, you nurture your soul's light.

These boundaries communicate: "You matter. Your essence is worthy of care." They foster a safe inner space where the soul can flourish.

Love for Others

Paradoxically, setting boundaries with love often improves relationships. When you are clear about your needs and limits, you communicate honestly and respectfully.

Others learn to trust your authenticity, and mutual respect grows. Boundaries prevent burnout, resentment, and misunderstanding—creating healthier, more loving connections.

Common Barriers to Setting Boundaries

Despite their importance, many hesitate to set boundaries due to fear, guilt, or cultural conditioning.

Fear of Rejection or Conflict

We fear that saying "no" will push others away or spark disagreement. But boundaries set from love are not about control or punishment—they are about clarity and respect.

True connection can withstand honest communication.

Guilt and People-Pleasing

Guilt often arises from childhood conditioning or social expectations that value self-sacrifice. Yet, sacrificing your well-being is neither sustainable nor kind.

People-pleasing neglects your inner team and ultimately disrespects both you and others.

Unawareness of Boundaries

Sometimes, we simply do not know where our limits lie. We may have blurred or ignored boundaries for so long that we must relearn to recognize them.

This is a process that requires patience and compassion.

How to Set Boundaries with Love

Step 1: Clarify Your Limits

Reflect on what feels manageable and nourishing for your body and soul. Define your needs clearly.

Example: "I need to rest by 9 PM to honour my body's need for sleep."

Step 2: Communicate Clearly and Kindly

Express your boundary honestly without apology or defensiveness.

Example: "I appreciate your invitation, but I won't be able to join tonight because I need quiet time to recharge."

Step 3: Practice Saying No

"No" is a complete sentence. Practice it gently but firmly. You do not owe lengthy explanations or justifications.

Step 4: Notice and Adjust

Boundaries are not fixed; they evolve with your needs. Pay attention to how your boundaries feel and adjust them as necessary.

Step 5: Hold Compassion for Yourself and Others

Setting boundaries may cause discomfort initially—for you or those around you. Offer patience and kindness in these moments, knowing that love underpins your actions.

Boundaries as Sacred Rituals

Transform boundary-setting from a chore into a sacred ritual by:

- **Creating physical symbols**: A special bracelet, a candle, or a ritual that signals your commitment to honour your limits.
- **Journaling about boundaries**: Reflect on how setting a particular boundary felt and the impact it had.
- **Breathing into boundaries**: Use deep breath to calm fear or anxiety before asserting a boundary.

These rituals deepen your connection to your inner team and your commitment to self-respect.

When Boundaries are Challenged

Expect resistance—both internally and externally—when you begin to set boundaries with love.

Internal Resistance

The mind may argue, "I must do this," or "I don't deserve rest." The body may resist change, and the soul may fear abandonment.

Meet this resistance with curiosity and kindness. Ask what fears or beliefs underlie the hesitation. Gently remind yourself of your worth and right to care.

External Resistance

Others may test your boundaries or react emotionally. Stand firm in your truth with grace, remembering that their reactions are their own.

You are not responsible for others' feelings but for your own integrity.

Boundaries as Freedom

Paradoxically, boundaries liberate rather than confine.

When you honour your limits, you create a container of safety from which you can fully engage with life. You free your energy to devote to what truly matters and cultivate deeper relationships rooted in honesty.

Boundaries foster freedom to be your authentic self without apology.

A Final Reflection

To set boundaries with love is to embark on a lifelong dialogue with your body and soul, a sacred practice of self-respect and courage.

It is an act of friendship, a tender yes to yourself that reverberates through every moment of your life.

May you come to know the profound peace and power that arise when you honour your limits with love — and in doing so, nurture the wholeness of your being.

THIRTY-THREE

THE GIFT OF BOUNDARIES

In the grand symphony of existence, the ability to set boundaries is a rhythm essential to the harmony of life itself. These boundaries are not harsh barricades but sacred lines, tenderly drawn with the ink of self-awareness, clarity, and, most importantly, love. They mark the contours of our being — the sacred space where our body and soul begin and end, where respect for ourselves first takes root.

To set boundaries is to engage in a sacred conversation with our inner world, listening attentively to the whispers of our body, the murmurings of our soul, and responding with kindness and courage. It is a dance of Honouring limits—not as restrictions imposed to punish or exclude, but as affirmations of self-respect, acts of compassion that nurture the wholeness of our being.

The Gift and Misunderstanding of Boundaries

Boundaries are often misunderstood, seen through the lens of fear or societal expectation as selfishness or weakness. We live in a culture that venerates constant productivity, relentless giving, and self-neglect, where saying "yes" to everything is a badge of honour, and "no" is feared like a forbidden word. But this misunderstanding is a veil that clouds the profound truth about boundaries.

Boundaries are not barriers to connection; they are the very architecture that supports authentic relationship — with ourselves and others. They hold space for our bodies to rest and heal, for our souls to breathe and grow. Without them, we risk dissolving into exhaustion, resentment, or fragmentation, losing sight of who we are beneath the demands and expectations that crowd our lives.

The irony is that boundaries, when lovingly held, do not isolate; they invite true intimacy. They say, "This is who I am, this is what I need," and by doing so, invite others to show up fully, honestly, and with respect. Boundaries are the gestures through which we teach the world how to treat us—and in that teaching, we offer others permission to do the same for themselves.

Why Boundaries Matter: The Language of Body and Soul
For the Body: The Sacred Language of Limits

Our body is a living temple, a vessel carrying us through life with unfathomable wisdom. It speaks to us constantly, often through sensations that we either heed or ignore. Fatigue, pain, tightness, ease—all are messages from this wise temple. When we choose to honour these signals, setting limits that protect the body's health, we affirm a sacred alliance.

Consider how you feel after days of relentless work, when your limbs ache, your breath shortens, your mind clouds. This is the body's language telling you to pause, to nourish, to rest. Choosing rest over relentless striving is not a weakness; it is an act of reverence. Saying "no" to demands that drain you is a prayer offered to your body, affirming its dignity and needs.

Ignoring these signals—the persistent "I am tired," the subtle "This is too much"—is a form of silent violence. It teaches the body that its boundaries are negotiable, that its voice is secondary to external demands. Yet the body's limits are not obstacles but guides pointing toward life's sustainability.

For the Soul: Guarding the Sacred Space Within

The soul, delicate and profound, carries the essence of who we are beyond the physical. It craves moments of silence, solitude, and self-honesty. When we fail to protect this inner sanctuary—by overcommitting, by surrendering to the noisy world—we risk fragmentation and depletion.

Setting boundaries with love for the soul means choosing what nourishes its light and gently declining what dims it. It is an act of guarding the sacred fire, ensuring it does not burn out from neglect or overexposure.

The soul's whisper may come as a longing for solitude, a craving for creativity, or a simple desire to be heard without judgment. Honouring these whispers is an act of profound respect for the inner life that sustains us.

Recognizing Your Boundaries: A Practice of Self-Awareness

To set boundaries with love, we must first become intimate with our limits. This is a practice requiring patience, curiosity, and gentleness.

Tune Into Physical Signals

Begin by tuning your attention to your body's messages:

- When does your body feel light, expansive, and free?
- When does it feel heavy, tense, or constricted?
- What sensations arise when you say "yes" more than you can bear?

Notice how your body reacts not just to activities, but to people, places, and situations. Is there a tightening in your chest when you think of certain commitments? A sinking feeling in your stomach when asked for favours you cannot afford? These sensations are the body's way of marking where your boundaries lie.

Observe Emotional Responses

Emotions are often the emotional barometer of boundary crossing. Feelings such as irritation, anxiety, guilt, or resentment may signal that your limits have been tested or ignored.

Ask yourself:

- What emotions surface when I feel overwhelmed or taken for granted?
- When have I felt guilt or fear around saying "no"?

- How do I feel when I assert my boundaries and honour my needs?

The answers offer insight into patterns that may need re-evaluation and compassion.

Listen to the Soul's Whisper

The soul speaks with subtlety but persistence.

- What does your soul need to feel safe, expanded, and nourished?
- Which relationships and activities leave your spirit feeling energized versus depleted?
- How can you create daily rituals that protect your inner sacred space?

These questions cultivate a dialogue with your deepest self, clarifying where boundaries are most needed.

Boundaries as Acts of Love

If boundaries are framed solely as defensive or exclusionary, we miss their greatest gift. When understood as acts of love, boundaries become radiant invitations—gifts given to ourselves and those we care about.

Love for Your Body

Saying "no" to overwork, harmful habits, or toxic environments says: "I see you, body. I honour you. I will protect your health and vitality."

This loving attention transforms boundaries from limiting edicts into gentle guardians of wellbeing. Boundaries invite you to treat your body as the sacred vessel it is.

Love for Your Soul

Choosing solitude, creativity, and nourishment for the soul expresses: "You matter. Your light deserves care."

Such boundaries protect the essence of your being, allowing your inner fire to burn bright rather than flicker out under the weight of exhaustion or neglect.

Love for Others

Clear boundaries communicated with kindness invite healthier relationships. When you show others your authentic limits, you foster trust, respect, and mutual care.

Boundaries prevent burnout, resentment, and misunderstanding, transforming interactions into connections rooted in honesty and empathy.

Common Barriers to Setting Boundaries

Many resist setting boundaries because of fear, guilt, or societal conditioning.

Fear of Rejection or Conflict

The fear that saying "no" will lead to abandonment or conflict is deeply human. Yet boundaries set from love are not about punishment but about respect.

True connection can endure honesty. Relationships that crumble at the truth often lack the roots of trust and respect.

Guilt and People-Pleasing

Guilt is often a legacy of childhood or culture, teaching that self-sacrifice is virtue and self-care selfishness. Yet true kindness arises from wholeness, not depletion.

People-pleasing sacrifices your own needs and ultimately harms both you and those you seek to please.

Unawareness of Boundaries

Sometimes boundaries are unclear because they have been ignored or overridden for so long. Rediscovering limits is a process requiring compassion and patience.

How to Set Boundaries with Love: A Gentle Guide

Step 1: Clarify Your Limits

Reflect deeply on what feels manageable and nourishing for your body and soul.

Example: "I need to rest by 9 PM to honour my body's need for sleep."

Step 2: Communicate Clearly and Kindly

Speak your boundary with honesty and calm, without apology or defensiveness.

Example: "Thank you for the invitation. I won't join tonight because I need quiet time to recharge."

Step 3: Practice Saying No

"No" is a complete sentence. You don't owe explanations beyond your comfort.

Step 4: Notice and Adjust

Boundaries evolve. Notice how your boundaries feel and be willing to refine them.

Step 5: Hold Compassion for Yourself and Others

Setting boundaries can cause discomfort. Approach this with patience and kindness—for yourself and those around you.

Boundaries as Sacred Rituals

Transform boundary-setting into a ritual that honours your commitment to yourself:

- Wear a bracelet or carry a token that symbolizes your boundary.
- Journal about your experience, reflecting on feelings and lessons.
- Use mindful breathing to centre yourself before asserting a boundary.

These rituals deepen your connection to your inner wisdom and your resolve.

When Boundaries Are Challenged

Resistance is natural.

Internal Resistance

The mind may argue that you "must" do something, or that you "don't deserve" care. The body may resist change; the soul may fear loneliness.

Meet this resistance with curiosity. Ask what fears or beliefs lie beneath. Offer yourself gentle reassurance.

External Resistance

Others may test your limits or react emotionally. Stand firm, recognizing their reactions are not your responsibility.

Your integrity is your guiding light.

Boundaries as Freedom

Though paradoxical, boundaries liberate. By Honouring limits, you create safe containers from which you can engage fully in life.

They free energy for what truly matters and allow authentic self-expression without apology.

A Final Reflection

To set boundaries with love is a sacred, ongoing practice—a dialogue between your body, soul, and the world.

It is an act of friendship with yourself, a tender yes whispered across the expanse of your being.

May you come to know the peace and power that arise when you honour your limits with love, nurturing your wholeness and radiance in every breath and step.

THIRTY-FOUR

JOY AS YOUR BIRTHRIGHT

Joy is not a distant prize, earned through toil or a fleeting visitor gracing us when fortune smiles. It is not a trophy to be won after hardship, nor a commodity to be rationed out by circumstance. Rather, joy is the intrinsic essence of our being — the natural radiance that arises when we live in harmony with ourselves and the world around us. To reclaim joy as our birthright is to remember that it is woven into the very fabric of existence, awaiting our recognition, not our conquest.

The Misconception of Joy as a Reward

Modern life, shaped by achievement-driven narratives, often places joy at the end of a long, arduous path — a reward for success, discipline, or endurance. This conditioning suggests that joy is conditional, contingent on external accomplishments: a promotion, a relationship, a financial milestone. Yet, this view breeds a paradox. If joy is perpetually deferred until conditions are met, it becomes elusive, slipping further from reach even as we chase it more fervently.

Philosophers and sages across cultures have challenged this transactional view. The ancient Stoics, for example, taught that joy — or more precisely, a serene contentment — arises not from external goods but from inner virtue and acceptance. Buddhist teachings speak of joy as a byproduct of awakening to the impermanence of all things, an unshakable peace beyond pleasure and pain. Even the Enlightenment thinkers, despite their emphasis on reason and progress, recognized that happiness flourishes in a mind free from distraction and attachment.

The insight is clear: joy is not a prize at the finish line; it is a seed planted within us, ready to blossom when we tend to the soil of our being.

Joy as the Expression of a Connected Self

What does it mean to say joy is an expression of a connected self? To understand this, we must explore the nature of selfhood and connection. The experience of joy emerges most vividly when the barriers between self and other dissolve — when we no longer see ourselves as isolated islands but as integral parts of a living whole.

Psychologists affirm that connection is fundamental to human flourishing. Our brains are wired for sociality; our emotional and cognitive well-being depends on relationships that nurture and affirm us. Yet, connection extends beyond human interaction. It includes our relationship with nature, with our inner selves, and with the vast mystery that underlies existence.

When we are fragmented — emotionally disconnected, mentally scattered, or spiritually disengaged — joy feels distant or superficial. It is replaced by restlessness, dissatisfaction, or even despair. But when we cultivate a sense of wholeness — through mindfulness, authenticity, and compassion — joy naturally unfolds as a reflection of that unity.

This connected self is not a fixed identity but a dynamic process. It is the awareness that I am both distinct and intertwined; that my well-being is linked with the well-being of others; that life is a shared journey rather than a solo race.

The Birthright of Joy: Philosophical Foundations

Across philosophical traditions, joy is recognized as more than a mere emotion — it is a fundamental orientation toward life.

Joy in Ancient Wisdom

In the Indian tradition, the concept of *Ananda* describes bliss as the essential nature of the soul — a state of pure being beyond dualities. The Upanishads teach that beneath the fluctuations of pain and pleasure lies an eternal joy that is our true self, unchanging and infinite.

Similarly, in Taoism, joy arises from aligning oneself with the Tao — the natural flow of the universe. It is not forced or grasped but allowed to emerge when we live in harmony with the rhythms of nature.

The Greek philosopher Aristotle described *eudaimonia* — often translated as flourishing or well-being — as the highest human good. While it encompasses moral virtue, it is also characterized by a profound and lasting joy that comes from fulfilling one's true potential and living in accordance with reason and virtue.

Modern Philosophical Insights

Existentialists like Jean-Paul Sartre and Simone de Beauvoir remind us that joy is tied to freedom and authenticity. Despite the inherent absurdity and challenges of existence, we have the power to choose our attitude, to create meaning, and to embrace life fully. Joy, then, is a courageous affirmation of being itself.

More recently, philosophers of mindfulness and positive psychology have emphasized the cultivation of joy through presence and acceptance. Rather than chasing external stimuli, joy is found in appreciating the immediacy of experience — the warmth of sunlight, the sound of a child's laughter, the quiet breath of morning.

The Anatomy of Joy: Beyond Pleasure

It is important to distinguish joy from pleasure or happiness, which are often mistaken as synonyms but differ in depth and duration.

Pleasure is typically sensory, immediate, and fleeting: the taste of a sweet fruit, the comfort of a warm bath, the thrill of new excitement. While pleasurable experiences can enhance life, their transient nature means they cannot sustain a profound sense of joy on their own.

Happiness is sometimes understood as a state of satisfaction or contentment that may depend on external circumstances. It is often shaped by success, relationships, or material well-being, and thus subject to fluctuation.

Joy, however, is a deeper and more resilient state. It is an underlying current of aliveness and gratitude that persists even amid suffering or uncertainty. Joy arises not despite hardship but sometimes through it — when we find meaning in struggle or recognize the beauty in impermanence.

Psychologist Carl Jung described joy as a "presence that comes from the soul," a sign that the inner self is alive and integrated. The spiritual teacher Thich Nhat Hanh called it a "seed" that can be cultivated in the garden of the mind through mindfulness and loving-kindness.

Cultivating Joy: Practices Rooted in Connection

If joy is our birthright, how do we awaken it in daily life? The journey toward joy is not a linear path but an unfolding process of alignment with ourselves and the world.

Embrace Presence

Joy blossoms in the soil of presence. When we fully inhabit the moment, without distraction or judgment, we open to the richness of life as it is. Presence is not a passive state but an active engagement — noticing the colours of a sunset, feeling the texture of a leaf, savouring the breath as it enters and leaves the body.

Mindfulness meditation offers a powerful tool to cultivate presence. By gently returning the mind to the here and now, we dissolve the worries of past regrets and future anxieties that obscure joy.

Foster Gratitude

Gratitude is the lens through which joy becomes visible. When we recognize the gifts already present — the air we breathe, the love we receive, the lessons we learn — we shift from scarcity to abundance.

Gratitude practices, such as journaling or silent reflection, help reorient our attention toward what nurtures us, reinforcing a sense of connection and appreciation.

Cultivate Compassion and Connection

Joy deepens when shared. Acts of kindness, empathy, and service create bonds that transcend isolation. These connections nourish the heart and remind us of our shared humanity.

Compassion begins with self-kindness, extending from acknowledging our own struggles without judgment to embracing others with open arms.

Align with Purpose and Meaning

Living in accordance with our values and purpose provides fertile ground for joy. When our actions reflect who we truly are, joy becomes an expression of authenticity.

This alignment may require reflection, courage, and sometimes change. Yet, the peace and joy that emerge are profound and sustaining.

Accept Impermanence

Joy is not about clinging to permanence but embracing change. The wisdom of impermanence teaches us to savour moments fully, knowing they are transient.

Paradoxically, this acceptance heightens joy because it awakens us to the preciousness of life's fleeting beauty.

Joy in the Face of Suffering

One of the most profound lessons is that joy and suffering are not opposites but companions on life's journey. To claim joy as a birthright is not to deny pain but to find the capacity to live fully despite it.

The great mystics speak of a "joy beyond sorrow" — a luminous presence that coexists with grief. Viktor Frankl, survivor of the Holocaust and founder of logotherapy, observed that even in the darkest conditions, humans retain the freedom to choose their attitude and find meaning, which can lead to joy.

When we make space for sorrow without resistance, joy can emerge as a deeper, more resilient light.

Joy as a Revolutionary Act

In a world often marked by division, injustice, and despair, embracing joy can be a radical act of resistance. It is a declaration that life is worth celebrating, that hope persists, and that love remains powerful.

Joy fuels creativity, courage, and connection. It inspires us to build communities rooted in kindness and respect, to nurture the earth, and to envision a better future.

By reclaiming joy as our birthright, we participate in a collective awakening — a renewal of the human spirit.

A Final Reflection: Returning Home to Joy

Joy is not something to be found "out there" but to be remembered within. It is the original song of the soul, waiting to be heard beneath the noise of doubt and distraction.

To live joyfully is to live authentically, vulnerably, and with open-hearted courage. It is to dance with life's complexities without losing sight of the light that shines through all.

May you come to know joy as your birthright — a steady flame that guides you home to yourself, and through you, lights the way for others.

THIRTY-FIVE
THE DAILY CHECK-IN

In the rapid currents of modern life, where demands, distractions, and duties swirl relentlessly, we often lose touch with ourselves. We hurry through days, carrying burdens that grow heavier because we do not pause to listen deeply. Yet, within us lies a wellspring of wisdom, a living dialogue between body and soul, waiting patiently for our attention.

The practice of the daily check-in—asking "Body, how do you feel? Soul, what do you need?"—is deceptively simple, yet profoundly transformative. It invites us to reconnect with the essence of our being, to cultivate self-awareness, and to align our actions with our true needs. In this chapter, we will explore the philosophy behind this daily ritual, its implications for well-being, and how it can serve as a compass guiding us toward balance, presence, and authenticity.

The Fragmentation of Modern Selfhood

To understand the power of the daily check-in, we must first consider the fragmentation that characterizes much of contemporary existence. We live in a world that values productivity, efficiency, and external achievements. Our identities are often constructed through roles—worker, parent, friend, citizen—while the inner dimensions of our body and soul are neglected or silenced.

The body, the most immediate and tangible aspect of ourselves, is often reduced to a machine to be optimized, controlled, or ignored until illness forces attention. We neglect its messages—fatigue, tension, hunger, pain—because acknowledging them might slow us down or disrupt our plans.

The soul, the realm of our deepest longings, values, and purpose, is often relegated to the background. It whispers through feelings of restlessness, yearning, or dissatisfaction, but we may confuse these signals for mere mood swings or psychological noise. We fill the void with distractions—screens, substances, busyness—avoiding the discomfort of introspection.

This disconnection from body and soul leads to a sense of alienation, burnout, and existential emptiness. We become strangers to ourselves.

The Daily Check-In: A Practice of Reconnection

The daily check-in is an intentional pause — a sacred moment to turn inward and listen with presence and compassion. It is a question posed in kindness, not judgment; an inquiry made with curiosity, not demand.

Asking the Body: "How Do You Feel?"

The body is our first home, the vessel through which we experience the world. It holds memories, emotions, and wisdom often inaccessible to the intellect. To ask the body how it feels is to tune into this living landscape — sensing tension, relaxation, warmth, cold, hunger, thirst, or pain.

This practice is not about diagnosing or fixing but about awareness. It honours the body as a trusted guide, an ally that communicates through sensations. By checking in, we learn to recognize signs of stress before they manifest as illness, to respond to needs for rest or movement, and to cultivate gratitude for the miraculous functioning that sustains life moment by moment.

Philosophically, this aligns with embodied cognition — the understanding that mind and body are intertwined, each influencing the other. The body is not a mere vessel but an active participant in shaping consciousness.

Asking the Soul: "What Do You Need?"

The soul's language is subtler, often expressed through feelings, intuitions, and longings. To ask the soul what it needs invites us to access our inner depths — to discern whether we seek creativity, connection, solitude, forgiveness, or meaning.

Unlike the body's more immediate signals, the soul's needs may require patience and reflection. It may respond through dreams, art, moments of stillness, or encounters with nature.

This inquiry cultivates alignment with our authentic self. It encourages us to live not just for external approval or survival but in harmony with our values and aspirations. The soul's needs are often the compass toward growth and fulfilment.

Philosophical Foundations of Self-Inquiry

The practice of asking questions to oneself has roots in various philosophical and spiritual traditions.

Socratic Method: The Power of Questioning

Socrates famously proclaimed, "The unexamined life is not worth living." His method of questioning aims to uncover truth through dialogue. While Socratic inquiry often involves external discourse, the same principle applies inwardly: self-questioning awakens awareness and challenges assumptions.

The daily check-in is a form of inner Socratic dialogue — a gentle, ongoing examination of our present state, promoting clarity and wisdom.

Mindfulness and Presence

Eastern philosophies emphasize the importance of presence and awareness of the here and now. The Buddha taught that suffering arises from ignorance of the present moment and attachment to desires.

By asking how our body feels and what our soul needs, we practice mindfulness—bringing attention to the present without judgment. This awareness fosters peace and reduces suffering.

Existentialist Reflection

Existential philosophers highlight the importance of authenticity and confronting one's own existence. Jean-Paul Sartre and Martin Heidegger emphasized "being-toward-death" and the need to own our choices.

The daily check-in encourages such ownership by asking us to face honestly what we need to live meaningfully, rather than drifting in distraction or conformity.

The Practical Benefits of the Daily Check-In

While the practice is philosophical, it yields tangible benefits in daily life.

Enhancing Self-Awareness

Regular check-ins develop the habit of introspection, helping us recognize patterns in our physical and emotional states. This awareness empowers us to make healthier choices, prevent burnout, and nurture well-being.

Building Emotional Resilience

By acknowledging what we feel and need, we validate our experiences instead of suppressing them. This fosters emotional resilience—an ability to cope with challenges without being overwhelmed.

Strengthening Mind-Body Connection

The practice bridges mind and body, reducing dissonance and fragmentation. When body and soul are heard and honoured, we become more integrated and whole.

Aligning Actions with Needs

Often, our actions are automatic or dictated by external demands. The daily check-in invites deliberate alignment — adjusting plans, setting boundaries, or engaging in restorative activities based on real needs.

Cultivating Compassion for Self

The tone of the check-in is important. It must be kind and curious, not critical. This cultivates self-compassion, which is essential for mental and spiritual health.

How to Practice the Daily Check-In

The simplicity of the practice is part of its power. It can be adapted to fit any lifestyle or belief system.

Step 1: Find a Quiet Moment

Begin with a moment of stillness. This could be first thing in the morning, before sleep, or any pause during the day.

Step 2: Ask the Body

Gently direct your attention to your physical self. Notice sensations without judgment. Ask silently or aloud, "Body, how do you feel?" Allow whatever arises to be present.

You might feel tired, tense, relaxed, or energetic. You might sense specific areas of discomfort or ease. Simply observe.

Step 3: Ask the Soul

Turn your awareness inward to your inner self. Ask, "Soul, what do you need?" Listen with openness.

The answer may come as a feeling, image, memory, or word. It may be a desire for rest, creativity, connection, or something deeper.

Step 4: Reflect and Respond

Take a moment to reflect on the responses. What actions, if any, can you take to honour these needs?

This could mean drinking water, stretching, taking a break, journaling, reaching out to a friend, or simply resting in the awareness.

Step 5: Close with Gratitude

Express gratitude for your body and soul — for their constant presence and wisdom.

Common Challenges and How to Overcome Them

Distraction and Restlessness

Our minds may resist slowing down, jumping to worries or tasks. Cultivating patience and gently returning attention to the inquiry helps.

Unfamiliarity with Inner Signals

For those unaccustomed to introspection, it may be difficult to identify feelings or needs. Journaling, meditation, or guidance from a counsellor can support development.

Judgment or Criticism

We may harshly judge our feelings or needs as "wrong" or "weak." Cultivating a non-judgmental stance is key to trust and openness.

Inconsistency

Like any habit, daily check-ins require commitment and kindness toward oneself if missed. Even sporadic practice brings benefit.

The Check-In as a Gateway to Deeper Self-Knowledge

The daily check-in is an entry point, a door opening toward richer self-awareness. Over time, this practice deepens, revealing layers of complexity and subtlety in our inner landscape.

It invites us to recognize the interplay between body, emotions, thoughts, and spirit. We begin to perceive how stress in one area affects the others, how unmet needs manifest physically or emotionally, and how healing is a holistic process.

This awareness fosters integration and balance. We cease to be fragmented selves chasing external goals and become unified beings living in alignment.

The Check-In and the Flow of Life

Life flows in cycles—of energy and rest, activity and stillness, joy and sorrow. The daily check-in attunes us to these rhythms. By listening to our body and soul, we learn to dance with life's changing tides rather than resist them.

This flexibility enhances adaptability and grace. We no longer strive against ourselves but move in concert with our own nature.

The Check-In as an Act of Self-Love and Radical Presence

To pause and ask "Body, how do you feel? Soul, what do you need?" is an act of profound self-love. It is a declaration that we matter, that our inner world deserves attention and care.

It is also an act of radical presence — a commitment to be with ourselves fully, without avoidance or denial.

This presence deepens our relationship with life itself, opening space for joy, peace, creativity, and healing.

The Ripple Effect: From Self-Care to Collective Care

Our relationship with ourselves shapes our relationships with others. When we listen deeply to our own body and soul, we cultivate empathy and patience. We become more attuned to the needs of others and the environment.

The daily check-in thus has a ripple effect, nurturing not only personal well-being but collective harmony.

A Final Meditation

To close this chapter, pause now. Take a deep breath. Ask softly:

Body, how do you feel?

Notice your answer, without rushing.

Soul, what do you need?

Sit in the space of your response, honouring whatever arises.

Offer gratitude to your body and soul for their constant presence, wisdom, and love.

May this simple practice guide you daily, leading you home to yourself and opening the path to a life lived with presence, purpose, and joy.

THIRTY-SIX

Your Inner Child is Still Watching

Within each of us, beneath the layers of adulthood, experience, and social masks, there resides a child—our inner child. This child is not a mere memory or a symbolic relic of the past but a living presence within us, quietly observing, feeling, and seeking. The inner child watches still, yearning for safety, love, and acknowledgment. To ignore this tender part is to live fragmented, incomplete. To nurture it is to open the door to wholeness, healing, and profound self-acceptance.

In this chapter, we embark on a philosophical journey to understand the inner child, explore why it still watches, and consider how embracing this child with compassion transforms our relationship with ourselves and the world.

The Inner Child: A Presence Beyond Time

The notion of the inner child has been explored in psychology, spirituality, and philosophy. It represents the primal essence of who we were as children—the source of wonder, creativity, innocence, and vulnerability. Yet, the inner child also carries the imprints of early experiences, wounds, and unmet needs.

Philosophically, the inner child is the dimension of our being that is closest to raw existence, before the intellectual mind layered itself with judgment, defense mechanisms, and societal conditioning. It is the part of us that still remembers what it was like to feel small, exposed, and dependent.

The phrase "Your inner child is still watching" is a call to awareness. It reminds us that, no matter how mature or successful we appear, this child remains present inside, waiting—not as a ghost of the past but as a vital part of our current self.

Why Is the Inner Child Still Watching?

The inner child watches because it is fundamentally concerned with survival and belonging. In infancy and childhood, we depend utterly on others for safety, nourishment, and love. When these needs are met with consistent care, the child grows with trust and confidence. But when needs are unmet, ignored, or violated, the child remains vigilant, watching for signs of danger or rejection.

Even if we have grown into independent adults, the memories and emotions of that child remain active in our subconscious. They influence how we respond to stress, intimacy, and self-worth. The inner child's gaze is a silent plea for reassurance: "Are you safe now? Am I loved? Will I be cared for?"

Ignoring this gaze is to deny an essential aspect of ourselves. It risks perpetuating inner conflict, emotional pain, and patterns of self-sabotage. But when we turn toward the inner child with openness, we offer the safety and love that were missing, allowing healing to begin.

The Inner Child and Authenticity

The inner child embodies authenticity. It is unfiltered by social expectations, cultural norms, or self-imposed limitations. This child expresses pure emotions—joy, fear, sadness, curiosity, and wonder—without the layers of adult rationalization.

To reconnect with the inner child is to reclaim authenticity. It means allowing ourselves to feel deeply, to play, to dream, and to be spontaneous. It means shedding the armour of perfectionism, control, and judgment.

Philosophically, this resonates with the existential call to live genuinely—to confront the world as we are, not as we pretend to be. The inner child invites us to honour the truth of our emotions and experiences, no matter how messy or imperfect.

The Inner Child as Guardian of Creativity and Play

Creativity springs from the well of the inner child. Children are natural creators, inventors, and explorers. They approach the world with fresh eyes and an open heart. However, as adulthood encroaches, the pressure to conform and produce "useful" outcomes often stifles this creativity.

Nurturing the inner child reignites our creative spark. It encourages playfulness—the freedom to experiment, fail, and imagine without fear of judgment. Play is not frivolous but essential to our mental and spiritual health. It refreshes the mind, heals wounds, and connects us to a sense of possibility.

Philosopher Friedrich Schiller once wrote that "man plays only when he is in the fullest sense of the word a man," highlighting the link between play and true human flourishing.

The Inner Child and Emotional Healing

Many emotional wounds originate in childhood—fear of abandonment, shame, rejection, or neglect. These wounds often remain hidden, buried beneath layers of coping strategies. The inner child holds these wounds as if they were scars on the soul.

Healing the inner child involves acknowledging and comforting these wounds rather than repressing or dismissing them. It is an act of radical self-compassion. Carl Jung described this process as individuation—the journey to integrate all parts of the self into a harmonious whole.

When we sit with the inner child's pain, listen to its fears, and offer reassurance, we dissolve shame and fear. We learn that the child is not alone, that it is seen and loved. This healing ripples outward, transforming how we relate to others and ourselves.

The Practice of Nurturing the Inner Child

Nurturing the inner child is not a one-time event but an ongoing commitment. Here are some ways to cultivate this relationship:

1. Listen Deeply

Create moments of quiet to connect inwardly. Imagine yourself as a compassionate guardian gently asking the child within, "What do you feel? What do you need?" Listen without rushing or judging.

2. Validate Emotions

Acknowledge the child's feelings as real and important. Whether it is sadness, anger, or joy, give space for expression. Remember, emotions are the language of the soul.

3. Provide Safety

Reassure the child that it is safe now. You are here to protect and care for it. This may be through visualization, affirmations, or physical gestures such as hugging yourself or holding your hands.

4. Encourage Play

Allow yourself time for playful activities that bring joy—drawing, dancing, storytelling, or simply daydreaming. Play reconnects you to the child's natural vitality.

5. Set Boundaries

Part of nurturing is also protecting the child from harm. Establish boundaries in your life that honour your needs and prevent abuse or neglect, whether from others or yourself.

6. Seek Support

Sometimes nurturing the inner child requires external help—therapy, supportive relationships, or spiritual guidance. Seeking help is a sign of strength and care.

The Inner Child and the Adult Self: An Ongoing Dialogue

Our relationship with the inner child is a dynamic dialogue. The adult self has the capacity for reason, perspective, and choice. It can hold the child with tenderness while guiding and protecting.

Philosophically, this relationship mirrors the ancient idea of the self as multiplicity—a composite of voices and facets rather than a singular identity. To be whole is to integrate these voices harmoniously.

When the adult self listens and responds lovingly to the inner child, it fosters integration and maturity—not by silencing or dismissing the child but by embracing it fully.

The Consequences of Neglecting the Inner Child

When the inner child is ignored or denied, several consequences may arise:

- **Emotional Fragmentation:** Feelings of emptiness, numbness, or unresolved pain persist.
- **Self-Sabotage:** Unconscious patterns of behaviour emerge, often rooted in childhood wounds.
- **Difficulty with Intimacy:** Fear of vulnerability and trust hinders relationships.
- **Chronic Anxiety or Depression:** Unaddressed inner turmoil can manifest as mental health challenges.
- **Loss of Joy and Creativity:** Life feels dull, mechanical, or devoid of wonder.

Recognizing these signs is a first step toward healing.

The Inner Child and Forgiveness

Often, the inner child carries blame and resentment—toward caregivers, circumstances, or even oneself. Forgiveness, both of others and self, is a powerful medicine.

Forgiveness does not mean forgetting or excusing harm. Rather, it is a release of the toxic burden that impedes healing. When we forgive, we free the inner child from the prison of past pain, opening space for peace and growth.

The Inner Child as a Guide to Self-Love

Ultimately, nurturing the inner child is an expression of self-love. It is a radical acceptance of all parts of ourselves—the bright and the broken, the joyful and the wounded.

This self-love is not narcissism or vanity but a deep recognition that we are worthy of care and kindness. It grounds us in a sense of belonging to ourselves, which is the foundation for authentic connection with others.

Philosopher Simone Weil said, "Attention is the rarest and purest form of generosity." To give attention to the inner child is to offer this pure generosity to oneself.

An Invitation: Meet Your Inner Child

Close your eyes for a moment. Picture yourself as a child—perhaps at a moment when you felt alone, scared, or misunderstood. See this child clearly. Notice its eyes, its posture, its expression.

Now imagine approaching this child with gentle kindness. What would you say? How would you hold it? What does this child need to hear from you today?

Feel the presence of your inner child watching, waiting, trusting you.

The Path Forward

The journey with your inner child is lifelong. It requires patience, courage, and compassion. Yet it is also a source of profound joy and transformation.

As you nurture this child within, you reclaim parts of yourself lost or hidden. You awaken creativity, deepen your capacity to love, and find a wellspring of resilience.

Remember: Your inner child is still watching, and it needs your love—today, tomorrow, and always.

THIRTY-SEVEN
GRIEF, LOSS, AND SELF-LOYALTY

Grief is a profound teacher. It is the shadow cast by love, the silent echo left by absence. In losing what we hold dear, we are stripped bare, confronted with the essential truth that all external things are impermanent. The faces, places, relationships, roles, and possessions we treasure are fleeting. Yet beneath this ephemeral surface, one companion endures: the self within.

This chapter is an invitation to explore grief not only as a painful passage but as a portal to deeper self-awareness and loyalty to the inner being. Through grief, we learn that the only permanence in life lies within us. This realization calls us to a radical fidelity—to become our own steadfast ally and sanctuary in the face of loss.

The Nature of Loss and Its Inevitability

Loss is an intrinsic part of the human condition. From birth, we are caught in the flow of change. People come and go, seasons shift, our bodies age, and circumstances evolve. To live fully is to embrace impermanence, and yet we resist it instinctively.

Philosophically, loss can be seen as a doorway—both feared and necessary. It shakes the foundations of our identity and challenges the illusions of permanence we often build our lives upon. It strips away the distractions and attachments, revealing the bare reality beneath.

The Buddhist teaching of *anicca*—impermanence—reminds us that all conditioned things are transient. Yet this awareness, though intellectually understood, becomes deeply real only when loss visits our own doorstep.

Loss carries with it grief, a complex emotional landscape of sorrow, longing, anger, confusion, and sometimes numbness. Grief is not linear; it ebbs and flows like the tide, unpredictable and unique to each individual.

The Inner Companion: A Permanent Presence

Amidst the turmoil of grief, there remains an unshakable presence—the inner companion. This is not a concept or an abstraction but the living core of your being: your consciousness, your awareness, your sense of 'I am.'

The external world changes, but this inner companion remains. It is the silent witness to joy and sorrow alike. It is the place where memories arise and fade, where emotions swirl and settle. It is the constant through the flux.

Philosophers and mystics across traditions have pointed to this inner presence as the essence of selfhood. It is not the roles we play, the titles we bear, or the possessions we accumulate. It is that which simply *is*—awareness itself.

Loss confronts us with the paradox of this inner companion. When everything else falls away, what remains? What can we truly count on? The answer is the self within—the seat of consciousness and being.

Loyalty to the Inner Self: What Does It Mean?

To be loyal to the inner self means to recognize and honour this permanent companion. It is an act of allegiance to the truth of who you are beneath circumstance.

Loyalty, in this context, is not a passive condition but an active commitment. It means:

- **Listening deeply** to your own needs and emotions, especially when grief clouds your vision.

- **Protecting your inner sanctuary** from the harsh judgments, self-blame, or external pressures that often accompany loss.
- **Nurturing your resilience** through compassion and self-care.
- **Accepting your vulnerability** without shame, understanding it as part of the human experience.
- **Standing as your own advocate**, especially when the world feels unkind or indifferent.

This kind of loyalty is revolutionary because it requires turning inward when instinct might urge us outward—to distraction, denial, or external validation.

Grief as a Mirror to the Inner World

Loss forces us to look inward. The external absence mirrors internal voids and longings. Grief reveals not only what we have lost but what we still carry inside—memories, feelings, unresolved questions.

In this way, grief can serve as a powerful teacher. It shows us the depth of our attachments and the intensity of our love. It teaches us about the human capacity to feel deeply, to endure suffering, and ultimately to heal.

Philosopher Soren Kierkegaard described grief as a "form of suffering" that tests the self but also refines it. Grief "unmasks" the illusions we live by and compels us to face the naked truth of existence.

The Paradox of Grief: Loss as Transformation

Though grief brings pain, it is also a catalyst for transformation. It strips away superficial identities and attachments, prompting a profound revaluation of self and life.

The loyal self—the inner companion—becomes the ground upon which renewal occurs. It is the seedbed of new meaning, new purpose, and new ways of being.

This transformation is rarely sudden or easy. It requires patience, honesty, and courage. It means sitting with discomfort, allowing tears and silence, and sometimes seeking solitude or support.

In embracing grief, we come closer to ourselves. We learn that loss, while heartbreaking, can be a passage to greater depth, wisdom, and authenticity.

The Role of Self-Compassion in Grief

Self-loyalty flourishes in the soil of self-compassion. To be loyal to yourself in grief means treating yourself with the same kindness you would offer a beloved friend.

Grief often stirs harsh self-judgment— "I should be stronger," "I should have done more," "I am broken." Such judgments only deepen the wound.

Self-compassion is the antidote. It invites us to soothe ourselves, to recognize our humanity, and to hold our pain tenderly.

Psychologist Kristin Neff defines self-compassion as comprising three elements: self-kindness, common humanity, and mindfulness. Together, these cultivate a supportive inner relationship, the essence of self-loyalty.

Cultivating the Inner Sanctuary

Grief invites the creation of an inner sanctuary—a safe mental and emotional space where you can retreat and renew.

This sanctuary is built through practices such as meditation, journaling, creative expression, or simply moments of quiet reflection.

It is a place where you can:

- Acknowledge your pain without fear.
- Connect with your inner companion with tenderness.
- Gather strength for the next step forward.
- Find clarity beyond the noise of external demands.

By returning regularly to this sanctuary, you strengthen your loyalty to yourself and deepen your resilience.

The Wisdom of Impermanence and Detachment

Philosophical traditions remind us that attachment to permanence is the root of suffering. The wisdom of impermanence does not mean indifference or detachment in a cold sense, but a compassionate acceptance of change.

When we understand that loss is natural and inevitable, we can approach grief with openness rather than resistance.

This acceptance deepens our loyalty to the inner self, which is not defined by external circumstance but by the unchanging presence beneath.

The Eternal Witness: Meditation on Presence

One way to anchor self-loyalty is through the practice of witnessing presence. When grief overwhelms, cultivating the ability to observe your thoughts and feelings without becoming entangled offers relief.

Imagine yourself as the eternal witness, observing the waves of grief rise and fall. You do not have to fight them or flee from them; you simply hold space for them.

This presence is your loyal self, steady and compassionate, a refuge in the storm.

Love Beyond Loss

Love does not end with loss; it transforms. The bonds formed through love endure in memory, in spirit, and in the very cells of our being.

When grief is honoured and processed, love remains a luminous thread that connects past and present.

Self-loyalty includes embracing this ongoing presence of love within yourself, a love that no absence can erase.

Practical Ways to Practice Self-Loyalty in Grief

1. **Daily Check-Ins:** Ask yourself, "How am I feeling today?" and "What do I need?" Listen deeply and respond kindly.
2. **Rituals of Remembrance:** Create personal ceremonies or moments to honour what has been lost and to celebrate the love shared.
3. **Journaling:** Write letters to yourself or the lost loved one, expressing emotions without censorship.
4. **Creative Expression:** Use art, music, or movement to channel feelings and reconnect with your inner companion.

5. **Seek Support**: Engage trusted friends, counsellors, or spiritual guides who respect your journey.
6. **Gentle Movement**: Walk, stretch, or practice yoga to reconnect body and mind.
7. **Rest**: Allow yourself time to rest and recover without guilt.

The Promise of New Beginnings

Grief closes one chapter but opens another. When we remain loyal to ourselves through grief, we emerge transformed—not as the same person but as one who has integrated loss into their being.

This is not forgetting but remembering differently—a memory infused with wisdom and acceptance.

The inner companion that watches is also the one that holds the promise of new beginnings. In its unwavering presence, we find the courage to face each day with openness and hope.

Closing Reflection: Your Eternal Companion

As you navigate grief, remember: the self within is your most faithful companion. This presence does not abandon, does not judge, and does not fail.

Honour this companion with loyalty—listen, protect, nurture, and love.

In doing so, you embody the deepest resilience: the ability to hold loss and love simultaneously, to grieve and to hope, to be broken and to be whole.

Grief may change you, but it cannot defeat the loyal self that lives eternally within.

THIRTY-EIGHT
WALKING YOURSELF HOME

To walk oneself home is a metaphor of profound depth. It is to journey through life's labyrinth, through all the winding roads of experience and emotion, only to arrive—finally—at the sanctuary of one's own true self. This chapter invites you to explore life not as a random unfolding of events or a chase after external goals, but as a sacred pilgrimage back to home: the place of self-acceptance, wholeness, and authentic truth.

The Meaning of "Home"

Home is more than a physical place. It is a state of being. A place of refuge where the heart finds rest and the mind finds clarity. The word "home" conjures images of comfort, safety, familiarity, and belonging. Yet, for many, the journey toward this home is obscured by illusion, distraction, and the pain of separation—from others, from life's circumstances, and from the self.

To walk yourself home is to recover this inner sanctuary, to shed the masks and burdens that have distanced you from your essence. It is a deliberate, conscious return to the place within where you are fully known and fully accepted.

The Journey of Life as a Path Back to the Self

Life, in its essence, is a path of return. Like the ancient hero who leaves the village only to come back transformed, each of us embarks on a pilgrimage not just outward into the world but inward toward our own being.

The philosopher Joseph Campbell spoke of the hero's journey—a mythic cycle of departure, trials, revelation, and return. But often the return phase is overlooked or undervalued. The greatest journey is the return home—walking back to oneself after all the wanderings.

This return is rarely linear. It is marked by detours of confusion, moments of despair, and phases of joy and growth. But its direction is always inward, toward wholeness.

Self-Acceptance: The Threshold of Home

At the heart of walking yourself home lies self-acceptance—the radical embrace of who you are in this moment, with all your imperfections, strengths, doubts, and gifts.

Self-acceptance is not complacency nor resignation. It is a courageous acknowledgment of reality without denial or self-condemnation.

Philosophers and spiritual teachers have long emphasized this acceptance as the foundation of true peace. When you accept yourself fully, you cease the exhausting battle of self-rejection and begin to live authentically.

To walk yourself home is to cross this threshold of acceptance.

The Illusions We Leave Behind

On the path home, we shed many illusions—false beliefs about who we should be, what we must achieve, and how others must perceive us.

We discard the masks worn to gain approval or avoid pain. These masks often separate us from our true self, leading to a fragmented existence.

Walking home requires peeling back these layers of pretense, exposing the raw but beautiful core beneath.

This process is both humbling and liberating. It can be painful but ultimately healing.

Wholeness as Integration

Home is wholeness. It is not perfection but integration—the harmonious coexistence of light and shadow within us.

Carl Jung spoke of the process of individuation, the lifelong journey of integrating all parts of the psyche to become a unified whole.

Walking yourself home means embracing your shadow—the fears, wounds, and contradictions that have been denied or hidden.

Wholeness arises not by rejecting these parts but by Honouring and understanding them, allowing them to be seen and held with compassion.

Truth as the Compass

Truth is the compass that guides you home. It is the inner knowing that points beyond illusion and distraction.

Truth is not a fixed doctrine but a living presence that unfolds as you deepen your awareness.

Philosophically, truth can be seen as that which aligns you with reality, with yourself, and with the world as it is—not as you wish it to be.

Walking yourself home means listening deeply to this inner compass, allowing it to steer your steps with courage and humility.

The Role of Presence

Presence is the vehicle by which we walk ourselves home. It is the practice of being fully here, fully now, with openness and attention.

To be present is to cease the endless distraction of mind-wandering and judgment, and to engage with life as it unfolds.

Presence is the sacred ground where acceptance, wholeness, and truth meet.

When you cultivate presence, you create space to encounter yourself without resistance.

The Challenges on the Path

The journey home is not without obstacles. Fear, doubt, and old conditioning can cloud the way.

There will be times when you feel lost, disconnected, or tempted to abandon the path.

These moments call for patience and self-compassion, recognizing that the journey itself is the teacher.

Each challenge is an invitation to deepen your commitment to yourself and to the walk.

Walking With Compassion for Yourself and Others

Walking yourself home is not a solitary endeavour. It calls for compassion—first toward yourself, then extending outward to others.

When you embrace your own struggles with kindness, you naturally develop empathy for the struggles of others.

Compassion softens the journey and enriches your understanding of interconnectedness.

It reminds you that everyone is on a path home in their own way.

Rituals and Practices to Support the Journey

Many traditions offer practices that support walking yourself home:

- **Mindfulness meditation** to cultivate presence.
- **Journaling** to explore inner landscapes.
- **Nature walks** to reconnect with simplicity and beauty.
- **Breathwork** to anchor awareness.
- **Reflective reading** of philosophy, poetry, and sacred texts.
- **Creating art or music** as expression of the inner journey.

These practices are not ends in themselves but tools to deepen your relationship with your true self.

The Moment of Arrival

What does it feel like to arrive home? It is a moment of profound peace, not because the world is perfect, but because you are no longer divided within.

It is the settling of restless seeking and the opening to quiet joy.

It is the recognition that you are enough, here and now.

Yet, the journey does not end with arrival. Home is both destination and ongoing presence. It is a living relationship with yourself, unfolding moment by moment.

Final Reflection: The Sacred Pilgrimage

To walk yourself home is to honour the sacred pilgrimage of life. It is a daily act of courage, presence, and love.

No matter how far you have wandered, you can always return. The path is open, waiting for your footsteps.

May you walk gently, with patience and grace, toward the true home within—where acceptance, wholeness, and truth reside.

THIRTY-NINE
BEYOND THE FINAL BREATH

The final breath—so often perceived as an ending, a closing of the physical chapter—holds a significance far beyond the surface of mortal departure. It is not the cessation of being, but a profound transition. The soul, the essence of who we are, continues beyond that last exhalation, journeying into realms unseen by the eyes of the living. To contemplate this transition is to confront the deepest mysteries of existence and to understand the sacred relationship between the body and the eternal spirit it carries.

This chapter invites a contemplative exploration into the nature of life and death, the continuity of the soul, and the reverence owed to the body as the precious vessel through which the eternal self experiences the temporal world.

The Illusion of Finality

Death, as a concept, often conjures fear, grief, and the unsettling unknown. It is taught to us as a boundary, the definitive end of our story. Yet, to those who seek deeper wisdom, death is not an end but a doorway. The final breath is a passage through which the soul leaves one realm and enters another.

Many spiritual traditions and philosophies affirm the soul's immortality—that which animates the body does not perish but transforms. Like a river flowing into the ocean, the soul merges with a greater whole, returning to a source beyond physical form.

The illusion of finality arises because our senses are limited to perceiving only the physical world. Beyond sight and touch lies a vast dimension of existence, where life continues in forms that defy ordinary understanding.

The Soul: Eternal and Unbound

The soul is often described as the essence of self, distinct from the transient body and fleeting emotions. It is the witness, the eternal presence behind the changing experiences of life.

Philosophers and mystics have long pondered the nature of this immortal essence. Plato envisioned the soul as an eternal traveller, temporarily housed in the body but never defined by it. The soul carries the memory of lifetimes, the imprint of wisdom, love, and growth accumulated across time.

This eternal self is not confined by the boundaries of the physical; it is unbound, timeless, and infinite.

Death as a Return, not a Loss

To those who see through the veil, death is a homecoming. It is a return to the origin, a reunion with the boundless source of being.

This perspective transforms grief into reverence. While the body may decay and the breath cease, the soul's journey continues with unbroken continuity.

Caring for the body, then, becomes an act of Honouring the sacred vessel that carries the soul through this temporary earthly sojourn. The body is not mere flesh; it is the temple, the vehicle, the embodiment of the eternal spirit in this life.

The Body as the Vessel of Eternity

The body is a marvel of complexity and resilience. It breathes, senses, moves, and expresses the infinite through finite form. It holds memory, emotion, and consciousness—the interface between soul and world.

To care for the body is to care for the vessel that allows the soul to experience, learn, and evolve. This care is an expression of respect for life itself, a recognition that every moment spent embodied is sacred.

The body's health influences the clarity of the mind and the openness of the heart, shaping the quality of the soul's earthly expression.

Living With Awareness of Mortality

Embracing mortality is not a morbid fixation but a profound liberation. Awareness of the impermanence of the body invites us to live more fully, to cherish each breath and sensation.

It softens attachments to material illusions and heightens appreciation for the present moment—the only true reality in which the soul dwells during its earthly sojourn.

To live consciously with mortality is to honour the sacredness of the body and the preciousness of time.

Rituals and Practices Honouring the Body and Soul

Throughout history, cultures have created rituals to honour the transition between life and death, reflecting deep respect for both body and soul.

- **Mindful breathing** connects body and spirit, reminding us of the sacred exchange of life energy.
- **Ceremonies of remembrance** celebrate the eternal nature of the soul.
- **Healing practices** such as massage, movement, and meditation nurture the body as a living temple.
- **Acts of compassion and service** honour the interconnectedness of all beings, reflecting the soul's boundless nature.

These practices cultivate an integrated awareness of life's cyclical nature.

The Continuity of Consciousness

Modern contemplative traditions and some branches of science explore consciousness as a fundamental aspect of reality, not merely a byproduct of brain activity.

The continuity of consciousness beyond physical death remains a profound mystery but one that many experiences and testimonies suggest is real.

Near-death experiences, spiritual visions, and deep meditative states reveal glimpses of an eternal dimension where love and awareness transcend time and space.

Caring for the Body: A Sacred Responsibility

Caring for the body is a sacred duty. It is an act of stewardship, a loving guardianship of the vessel through which the soul manifests.

Nutrition, rest, movement, and mindfulness are ways to honour this sacred trust. To neglect the body is to dishonour the eternal self that animates it.

By nurturing the body, we prepare it as a worthy vessel for the soul's journey—both in this life and in the transition beyond the final breath.

Death as Transformation and Invitation

Rather than fearing death, it can be embraced as a transformation—an invitation to shed the physical form and expand into greater freedom.

Death invites us to reflect on what truly matters: love, connection, integrity, and the legacy of the soul.

It calls us to release attachments and cultivate peace with the inevitable flow of life and beyond.

The Gift of Mortality

Mortality is a gift wrapped in paradox. It imbues life with urgency, depth, and meaning.

Knowing that our time in this body is limited can inspire a deeper connection to ourselves and others.

It can motivate us to live authentically, to express our truths, and to love without reservation.

Mortality calls us home—to presence, to essence, and to eternal being.

The Final Breath as Sacred Passage

The final breath is a sacred passage—a moment of profound transition and grace.

It is the closing of one chapter and the opening of another, a bridge between worlds.

Honouring this moment with compassion, presence, and respect elevates the soul's journey and comforts those who remain.

Reflection and Invitation

As you contemplate the mystery beyond the final breath, may you be inspired to honour your body as a precious vessel, to live with mindful awareness of your eternal essence, and to greet the journey of life and death with openness and grace.

May the understanding that your soul continues beyond this physical form bring peace to your heart and illuminate the path you walk.

FORTY

YOU WERE NEVER ALONE

In the vast expanse of our existence—through moments of joy, despair, growth, and surrender—there lingers a profound truth often overlooked: you were never alone. Not in the way solitude isolates, nor in the way loneliness fractures the spirit. Rather, from the very first breath you took, your body and soul have been your constant companions—intimate, unwavering, and eternal.

This final chapter brings together the threads woven throughout this journey. It invites you to recognize the lifelong presence of these two integral aspects of your being—the physical and the spiritual—and to embrace the profound solace and strength that comes from knowing they accompany you, now and beyond any temporal boundary.

The Illusion of Separation

Human life is often shadowed by the feeling of isolation. We perceive ourselves as separate entities, cast adrift in a world full of others, struggling to connect and be understood. This sense of separateness can feel so real, so visceral, that it shapes the entirety of our experience.

Yet, this perception is a veil—an illusion created by the mind's tendency to categorize, to divide, and to see difference instead of unity. The truth beneath the surface is that you have never been alone because the most fundamental companionship is within you.

Your body—this tangible, breathing presence—and your soul—the unseen, eternal essence—have been with you in every heartbeat, thought, and sensation. Together, they form a unity that transcends loneliness.

The Body: Your First and Closest Friend

Long before you understood the world, before your mind constructed ideas of self and other, your body was there. It cradled you, protected you, and carried you through infancy, childhood, and every stage of growth.

Your body is not a mere shell or vessel; it is your first home, your original friend. It speaks to you in subtle language—through aches, rhythms, and impulses—inviting you to listen deeply.

To be in your body is to be in presence, to connect with the moment unfolding. In every breath you take, your body anchors you to life itself. It carries your stories in its cells, remembers your joys and sorrows, and offers a constant reminder that you are here—alive and real.

This closeness is a source of companionship beyond measure. Your body is a living testament that you have never been alone because it never left you, never abandoned you, even when your mind or heart felt lost.

The Soul: The Eternal Companion

If the body is your closest friend in the realm of form, the soul is your eternal companion beyond it. The soul is that intangible spark within, the essence that transcends time and space, the part of you that is always whole.

Throughout your life, the soul witnesses your journey. It holds your deepest truths, your essence beyond labels and roles. The soul whispers to you in moments of quiet, calling you back to who you truly are.

Though unseen, the soul's companionship is as real and vital as the beating of your heart. It is a presence that neither time nor circumstance can diminish.

In your darkest hours, when you feel abandoned by the world, your soul remains—a steadfast light in the shadows, reminding you that you are never truly alone.

The Dance of Body and Soul

The relationship between body and soul is a sacred dance—a perpetual interplay that shapes your experience of existence.

Your body grounds you in the physical, allowing you to taste, touch, move, and feel. Your soul opens you to the infinite, to meaning, purpose, and connection beyond the tangible.

When you honour both, you live in balance—integrated and whole. Ignoring one for the other creates imbalance: too much focus on the body alone can lead to disconnection from deeper meaning, while neglecting the body can cause fragmentation and suffering.

Together, body and soul hold you in a circle of companionship that is unbreakable. They are not two separate entities but parts of a profound unity that sustains your being.

The Journey of Self-Discovery

To realize that you were never alone is to embark on a journey of self-discovery—one that reveals the depth of your own presence.

This journey is not about seeking external validation or searching for answers in the outside world. It is about turning inward, listening to the wisdom of your body, and tuning into the voice of your soul.

In silence, meditation, or simple awareness, you begin to notice the constant companionship within. The body's heartbeat, the breath's rhythm, the soul's quiet guidance—all become touchstones on your path.

This inward turning dissolves the illusion of isolation and reveals a sanctuary of wholeness.

Love as the Bridge

Love is the bridge that connects body and soul, self and other, the temporal and the eternal.

The love you carry for yourself—your body and your soul—is the foundation of all other love. It nurtures self-acceptance, compassion, and kindness.

This love heals wounds inflicted by loneliness and fear. It reminds you that companionship begins at home, within your own being.

When you cultivate love for yourself, you open the door to authentic connection with others, recognizing that their journey is also accompanied by their own eternal companions.

The Eternal Companionship Beyond Time

Time, like space, is a construct that shapes our experience but cannot confine the soul.

Your body is subject to time's passage—aging, changing, and eventually dissolving—but your soul transcends it.

This means that the companionship you share with your soul is timeless. It stretches beyond birth and death, beyond any boundaries that seem to define existence.

The soul remembers what the body forgets: that you are part of an eternal unfolding, a timeless dance of creation and return.

The Wisdom of Presence

Presence is the key to experiencing your companionship fully. When you are present, you feel the aliveness of your body, the depth of your soul, and the connection between them.

Presence is not a state to be achieved in the future; it is accessible now, in this moment.

By cultivating presence through mindfulness, breath awareness, or simple observation, you anchor yourself in the reality that you have never been alone.

The Healing Power of Acknowledgment

Acknowledging the companionship of your body and soul is healing.

It heals the wounds of abandonment and disconnection. It heals the fragmentation caused by neglect or self-rejection.

This acknowledgment is an embrace—a heartfelt recognition that you are complete and accompanied.

Healing arises when you listen with kindness to your body's signals and honour your soul's longings.

The Role of Community and Connection

While your most profound companionship is within, it is reflected and enriched through relationships.

Community is a mirror where you see aspects of your own companionship reflected back.

In authentic relationships, you recognize that others, too, carry their body-soul unity.

This shared human experience deepens your understanding that none of us is truly alone.

Facing Life's Challenges Together

Life's challenges—pain, loss, uncertainty—can make solitude feel unbearable.

Yet, it is precisely in these moments that your internal companionship shines brightest.

Your body holds strength and resilience; your soul holds wisdom and peace.

Together, they walk with you through every trial, offering support beyond words.

Embracing Your Wholeness

To end this journey is to embrace your wholeness: body and soul, form and essence, temporal and eternal.

You are not fragmented or incomplete. You are a unified being with constant companionship.

This truth frees you from fear, loneliness, and separation.

The Invitation

As you close this book, take a moment to feel the presence within.

Place a hand on your heart or belly, and acknowledge the body that has carried you.

Close your eyes and sense the soul that witnesses all.

Whisper quietly: "I am not alone. I am whole."

May this truth be your guide, your comfort, and your strength.

You were never alone—and you never will be.

Afterword: A Gentle Return

You have walked through the pages of this book, not as a student, but as a soul remembering its own truth. Perhaps you've found your breath again. Perhaps you've heard your own silence more clearly. Or perhaps you've simply paused long enough to feel your body in a new way.

Wherever this journey has taken you, remember: there is no final destination—only a deepening. Your body will still wake with you each morning. Your soul will still whisper in the quiet. Let this companionship continue. Let it root you in presence, remind you of your worth, and carry you when the path feels uncertain.

You are not alone. You never were.

A Letter To The Reader

Dear Companion,

Thank you for opening this book and allowing these words to become a part of your inner world. Whether you read it slowly or in a single breath, know this: it was written with reverence for your life, your story, your sacred unfolding.

If something here spoke to you, I invite you to carry it gently. Let it guide you to moments of stillness, clarity, and compassion.

And if you ever forget your way—start again with a question:

"Body, how do you feel?"

"Soul, what do you need?"

With deep gratitude,

Titus Nazarene Kujur

Daily Practices To Stay Connected

You don't need grand rituals to return to yourself. Just small, consistent gestures. Here are a few you can carry into everyday life:

- Morning Check-In: Place your hand on your heart. Breathe. Ask: How do I feel today?
- Sacred Space: Light a candle or sit quietly for five minutes with no agenda.
- Soul Journaling: Write a single sentence beginning with "Today, my soul longs for…"
- Body Care Reminder: Hydrate, rest, stretch, nourish—your body is your sacred vessel.
- Evening Gratitude: Before sleep, name one thing your body or soul carried well today

Acknowledgments

To the body—resilient, tender, and wise.
To the soul—silent, luminous, and enduring.
And to every reader who chooses to walk this path of remembering—you are the reason this book was written.

To those who held space for this work—editors, friends, early readers, and loved ones—thank you. Your encouragement turned quiet thoughts into pages.